The
Project

Dr. A. Arrington

Copyright © 2016 Dr. A. Arrington

Edited by: Mariah Patterson

Published by Project Theme ©

All rights reserved.

ISBN-13: 978-1530831227
ISBN-10: 1530831229

DEDICATION

To my two very best friends in the whole world: my wonderful
and inspiring boys. Thanks for your support, input and the
sacrifice of quality time. I love you more than I love you!

CONTENTS

ACKNOWLEDGMENTS

Thanks to everyone who supported me through this journey.

1 THE INTERVIEW

I sat poised in my seat, behaving in a manner more sophisticated than I actually was in my more personal life.

"Mr. Boyd will be with you shortly," the receptionist recited as she probably had many times before.

I was guessing she spent her days reassuring those waiting in the lobby that they would soon be greeted by the lucky workforce members who sat in cubicles behind the infamous large door she guarded.

I was very excited to have an interview with one of the top IT firms in the metro area. I had convinced myself it was the result of my keen ability to embellish my skills on my very aptly prepared resume.

The interview actually began many weeks ago with a phone screen from the HR manager, followed by a second phone screen by Mr. Boyd. I chuckled to myself as I remembered desperately searching my notes for answers while sitting stuffed in my hot car hiding from my coworkers and most importantly my boss.

In the later weeks, I had spoken with other project managers on Mr. Boyd's staff, who asked me situational questions regarding my past experience and how I would deal with common issues as a project manager within their company.

During those phone calls, I somehow managed to get around terms like SDLC, charters and gateways to make it to the in-person interview with Mr. Boyd.

Suddenly, the large door behind the receptionist opened and a handsome-looking man with salt and pepper hair strode through. He had no inkling of a smile and his presence demanded respect.

"You must be Joyce. Follow me," he said curtly.

"Thanks for taking the time to see me," I chimed with a winning smile I had been told was very beautiful.

He didn't respond, and I fell silent as I followed

Mr. Boyd's lead through a maze of very bland gray cubicles lightly decorated with personal photos and badges of accomplishment.

I glanced down at the carpet and found that it, too, was gray with specs of black and red. Not much color on the walls, floors or faces of those working behind double monitors.

As I sat in the seat Mr. Boyd motioned to, I made sure to carefully remove the meticulously-crafted resume from my leather portfolio to ensure no wrinkles garnished its contents and slid it over the large oak desk to a stern Mr. Boyd.

As he reviewed my resume, I recalled how my morale had dropped each day as I waited to hear about an actual in-person interview. The call to schedule an interview finally came, but was re-scheduled twice.

During the moments after my phone interview, I daydreamed about doubling my salary and leaving my dead-end administrative job where I was blindly promised advancement year after year with no results.

Mr. Boyd only looked up briefly before returning his eyes to the stapled mass of papers I considered a worthy document of my true ability.

Websites were ambiguous on how long was too long in terms of resume content. I thought it best to show longevity in my experience. While I did not have project management experience, per se, I found areas in my background that I felt could adequately persuade a potential employer to believe otherwise.

I was lucky to find my current job as a project administrator, supporting a PM that doubled as my mentor. While not the best mentor, she was a great PM and I managed to learn from her through my own efforts. But after three years and a completed degree, I was looking for a change.

"I see here that you worked on a large SAP project

that was gauged to generate revenue. How did you use EVM in order to manage the ROI for the project?" Mr. Boyd asked, looking up from my resume.

Why did his first question have to be so difficult? EVM? EVM? What was EVM? I, of course, could not pull out my notepad but I danced around the question, admitting that maybe I had not directly worked with it, but was sure the project manager in control had used it at some point while I supported the aforementioned project manager.

Mr. Boyd gave me a disapproving look before returning his eyes to my resume. He asked a few more scenario-based questions before telling me that they would be making a final decision at the end of the week.

I said a small prayer as I walked through the massive parking lot. I started the engine on my fifteen-year-old car and drove off with hopes that I would receive a call at the end of the week with good news.

I returned to my less than exciting job, thankful that I was able to work my interview in during my lunch break.

***

I was sitting at my desk searching the web for the best books to use to study for the PMP. I had gone on several interviews in the past and found PMP certification was highly desired in the project management field.

Mr. Boyd had made it clear about his intentions to require that all project managers on his team be certified in the project management professional certification.

"Where were you the other day?" Cindy asked, stopping by my small desk.

"I told you I had an interview," I whispered to my closest friend in and out of work.

I tried to hide my screen because Cindy was not in favor of me finding work elsewhere.

"I told you they are posting a job for a PM in my

department," Cindy whispered, lowering her head into my cubicle.

"Yes, but when? And how many people on your team will be clawing for that role?" I asked, sitting on my desk to fully cover my computer.

"Soon. Just sit tight and you will be the first to know when it's posted!" Cindy said in a low tone as she skipped away with a smile.

I sat down again and leaned forward on my desk cupping my cheeks in the palm of each hand and let out a big sigh.

I had just finished a very unsuccessful professional development meeting where my boss told me it may be another year before I could begin cross-training for the project manager position in my own department. If only someone would give me a chance.

I had more degrees and to be quite frank, more common sense than my boss and my boss' boss, but I was still being held back. All I wanted was to be recognized for my talents and be given the opportunity to grow and advance.

While I worked on my master's degree, I had complained to one of my professors about my experiences. I remembered my professor saying,

"It is important to remember that working for someone who is uninterested in advancement themselves will always work to hold you back."

While sitting in boredom, waiting for the end of the work day to come, I decided to join a highly recommended project management training website. It was filled with many helpful resources.

My current non-challenging role left me plenty of time to study and further prepare for a role I had wanted for a long time.

When my phone rang, I crossed my fingers and hoped it was a call from Mr. Boyd; instead, it was my perfect sister, Stacy.

I loved my sister, but hated speaking with her in moments when my life seemed like a failure. Stacy had a perfect job at the perfect company and to top it all off, the perfect guy.

"Hi, my sweet, darling sister, how are you?" I managed a slight smile. I had learned long before that by simply smiling, I could change my tone on the phone.

"I have someone I want you to meet," Stacy chimed in her bright, bubbly way.

"No thanks!" I shook my head fervently. "The last time you and Thad tried to hook me up, it was a disaster."

Thad was Stacy's perfect boyfriend. He was a professional businessman who worked at a big firm downtown.

"Just hear me out, Joycie. You know how you are always telling me you need a mentor? Well, there's this guy that works in Thad's office and he is one of the top performing project managers there. He has agreed to meet with you for lunch," Stacy sang. I could almost hear her jumping up and down.

"Oh has he?" I didn't want to appear ungrateful, but Thad and Stacy were always trying to secretly hook me up with men who were nothing like anyone I would date. It was one horrific ordeal after another.

"C'mon Joycie, just give the guy a chance," Stacy pleaded.

I rolled my eyes and thought about how uninterested I was in meeting one of Thad's friends; then I remembered that Mr. Boyd still had not called.

"Okay," I said quickly before telling Stacy I had to go, although I really had completed most of my work for the day.

***

It was a sweltering 90 degrees and I made the bad decision to wear one of my interview suits to meet with

Thad's friend. I checked the mirror in the lobby bathroom before signing in. It didn't hurt to look twice because he might be good looking after all.

After a quick call from the receptionist, it was not long before I was greeted by a short, slightly-balding guy, with coffee-stained teeth.

When Charles came out, I immediately recognized him. He had been in one of my PMP training courses.

"Joyce?" he asked with his hand reaching out. "You look oddly familiar."

"Hi," I said, reaching out my hand to shake his, with my perky, interview-like smile on my face. "The PMP study course."

"That's right. I'm Charles," he said, reminding me. "It's such a small world. So Thad dates your sister."

"Yep!" I said, standing with an awkward look on my face. "You have obviously gone a lot further than me since the course."

"Well, I was already a project manager, just a bad test taker," Charles said, smiling.

Charles wasn't cute or even somewhat handsome. He was just sort of plain. He couldn't have been much older than I was, but he certainly seemed to be aging faster.

Charles led me down a long corridor that eventually ended with partitions of cubicles that reminded me of Mr. Boyd's IT firm. At the end of a shorter hallway, Charles guided me into a medium-sized office with a nice view of the city.

"Have a seat," he said, motioning to a small, yet comfortable-looking chair.

His office was decent. Not too flashy and not too bare. There was a small bookshelf with a mixture of software and project management books. I could see myself in his chair.

"Tell me a little about yourself," he invited.

"I'm currently a project administrator and I don't have any experience as an actual project manager. It seems that all of the jobs out there want at least five years' experience. Frankly," I sighed, "I'm bored in my administrative role and I need to be challenged more."

I went on to tell Charles about my training classes and finishing my degree. I almost regretted mentioning my constant resume updates and dead-end interviews.

"Well, have you ever managed an event or planned a vacation?" Charles asked, tilting his head to the side.

"Yeah, but—" I started before Charles cut me off.

"Most people think they have never managed a project before, when they actually have done it multiple times. It's easy to apply project principles without even knowing it. For example, you probably created some type of plan, organized some activities or even created a budget," Charles said as he swiveled in his black leather desk chair.

"I never thought of it that way," I said, thinking of the many other times I could have used project management skills.

"Project management is simply the application of tools and techniques through the use of a defined process or method," Charles explained as I soaked everything in.

"How do you know which tools are best for any given situation?" I asked.

"Truth is, it depends. I know it sounds like a sloppy answer, but it's my favorite when it comes to project management. No two days are the same and no two projects are the same," Charles said, playing with a pen on his desk.

He was really engaged and it made me happy to know that he was trying hard to help me, even during our first meeting.

"I really appreciate you taking out the time to help me," I smiled.

"When I first got into project management I didn't have anyone to show me around and after studying for that exam, I wish I had. I'm busy, but I will do what I can to be a good mentor," Charles offered with sincerity. "That is, if you will have me?"

"Of course. I appreciate that." I thought of how nice it was of Charles to offer such kind words.

While I was taking out my notebook to take notes, Charles took a call. When he hung up, he had a bright smile on his face.

"What?" I said excitedly, sensing he had news for me.

"Either you are the luckiest girl I know or you simply have perfect timing," Charles responded, switching positions in his chair. "That was one of my close college buddies. He is actually looking for an entry level project manager to join his team."

I couldn't believe it.

"I'll take it!" I almost yelled.

"Slow down," Charles said, grinning at my enthusiasm. "It's not exactly in the bag. He'll want to interview you, of course, but I'm willing to take some time to prep you before you go in."

"Absolutely," I smiled. "Where does your friend work?"

"Some gaming company. It's rather large, I think."

I was filled with excitement. This could be the opportunity I was looking for all along. Charles promised to pass along my information to his friend and I promised Charles I would contact him to set up a prep session if I was offered an interview.

Charles, while not the attractive love nugget I was looking for, was very resourceful.

Charles' friend did not waste time contacting me to schedule an interview. This prompted multiple training sessions with Charles. He offered resume tips, quizzed me on project principles and gave me suggestions on how to win his friend over.

By the time the interview came, I was no longer worried that Mr. Boyd had never called, but I was ready to get the job with Charles' college buddy, Tracy Johnson.

I even splurged and purchased a brand new interview suit and resume portfolio to appear impressive.

I arrived at my interview with Tracy thirty minutes early. I sat in my car reviewing my resume and my notes. I took one last look through my PMBOK and closed it, throwing it in the back seat before heading inside. During my project management training course, the PMBOK guide had been recommended as quality reference material and I used it frequently.

When I entered the building, I was amazed at all the color and intriguing images. There were gigantic posters dangling from the high ceilings and large, decorative light fixtures in the lobby.

There were people walking around in blue jeans and tennis shoes with multiple badges hanging from their necks. There was color everywhere, including the receptionist's purple hair.

"I'm here to see Tracy Johnson." I stumbled over my words as my eyes darted from posters to lime green walls and casually dressed staff.

I glanced at the bright orange badge that read Game Over. During my sessions with Charles, I researched the company, but never would have expected the scene I was taking in.

I took my seat on a small art deco couch that looked minuscule against the large floor to ceiling windows.

"Hello, Joyce," said a young girl walking up, wearing jeans and a Game Over T-shirt.

"Yes. I'm here to see…"

"Tracy? Yes, I'm Ashli, his assistant. I'll be taking

you up."

As I walked through the building, I noticed open cubicles with chalkboard walls and computer monitors the size of large televisions.

I was seated in a conference room with a large monitor and an even larger frosted dry erase board. The conference table was garnished with orange plastic chairs.

This is fancy, I thought. My current office space was gray and drab with dim lighting, sectioned cubicles and white walls that reminded me of an insane asylum.

"Sorry. My meeting ran late." A tall and visibly athletic man entered with his hand outstretched.

I was so enthralled, I barely could remember to extend my hand to his.

"No. It's okay, I'm enjoying the view," I said, motioning to the high floor view of downtown.

"Yes it is a nice view," the man said. "I'm Tracy."

"Nice to meet you," I smiled.

"We've only just moved into this building a year ago. It does have its perks." Tracy began the interview as informally as I had ever experienced.

He explained that the company was new to project management and that he had started the Project Management Office or PMO a year ago when he joined as the director.

The organization decided the PMO was needed to help govern all of the new projects that were previously being managed by functional managers with no real methodical application.

He was working to build his team of project managers, but they mostly managed the projects associated with gaming development.

"As you can see," he continued, "we are a growing gaming company and we have a lot of great projects. We work long and hard, but we are rewarded."

I was excited to learn that they received daily

casual-dress days, free lunch in the onsite cafeteria, 17 paid vacation days, and access to a gaming lounge and exercise room. Not to mention, employees were immediately vested in the 401k plan and the healthcare was 100% covered.

"Those are some great benefits," I smiled.

I thought I was dreaming when Tracy explained that his current team worked using Agile methodology, but he needed someone with Waterfall experience to handle the non-technical projects that would be absorbed by his group. This meant I would get an opportunity to learn about both methodologies.

I worked really hard trying to remember what Charles told me during our sessions. I focused on speaking about the things I knew and was honest when Tracy mentioned something in which I was unfamiliar or had no past experience.

I felt very confident leaving the interview. As I climbed into my car, I said a long prayer and really hoped that this time I would get a call.

2 THE CALL

I sat at the bar in a half daze, thinking about all of the wonderful, inspiring things that Tracy had mentioned during the interview.

I was meeting Stacy and Thad for Happy Hour since we had all confessed to having a tough week.

"So I heard from Charles you had an interview," Thad said. "How'd it go?"

"I haven't heard anything, so fingers crossed," I said, crossing my fingers for added effect.

"How is Charles working out as a mentor? He can be really tough," Thad said, taking a swig of his drink.

"No. He's amazing. Thanks so much for arranging for us to meet. Without him, I would not have had an interview," I said, moving my glass of wine from one spot on the counter to another.

"Relax Joycie, and have some fun." Stacy danced as she grabbed Thad and started to move with him at the bar. It was clear her two drinks were starting to kick in.

"I think I'm going to go," I said, reaching for my wallet.

"You're such a buzz-kill," Stacy scoffed. Obviously, she was the younger and more adventurous sister.

I started to respond to Stacy when my cell phone rang. I did not recognize the number and wondered if it was a bill collector.

"Hello," I answered as I exited the bar.

"Hello, may I speak with Joyce Davis?" a man's voice asked on the other end.

Yep, it was a bill collector.

"Uh, this is she," I said, trying to remember how much I had in my savings account.

As I listened on, I learned I was speaking to Bill Adams on behalf of Mr. Boyd, who wanted to make an official offer of employment to join the team as a first level project manager. The salary would start at $85,000 per year.

I almost dropped the phone. That would more than double my salary.

"Thank you," was all I could think to say.

"I will send you the official offer letter by email and I will FedEx the hard copies for official signatures," Bill Adams continued, "and you have two weeks to accept or decline the offer."

"Okay," I said, trying to hold in my screams until I hung up the phone.

"What's going on?" Stacy asked, stumbling out of the bar.

"I got the job!" I squealed.

"She got the job!" My sister echoed me with her hands in the air. Then with a confused look, she asked, "Which one?"

"Does it matter?" I laughed.

"We have to celebrate," Stacy said as she pulled me

back into the bar.

As Thad ordered another round of drinks, I sat a little surprised, wondering what I had done to win over Mr. Boyd. *Perhaps he offered the job to someone else and they declined it,* I thought.

I wanted to call Charles and give him the good news, but Stacy didn't waste any time yanking me on to the dance floor for a celebratory dance and another drink, of course.

***

I got up early to get a jog in and clear my head. I was trying to decide if I should quit my job on the spot or give the proper notice. I didn't want to spend another day at that awful office, but I didn't want to burn any bridges either.

Two weeks' notice should do, I thought as I picked up the pace heading around a deep curve in the tree-lined park. I hadn't run that early since I got the project administrator job.

But after the job offer from Mr. Boyd, I felt refreshed and empowered. I stopped at a bench to rest. I was clearly out of shape.

It was nearing seven thirty and I thought I'd better head back home to get ready for work. Bending over to catch my breath, I heard a faint sound I almost recognized.

Realizing it was my cell phone, I opened the side pocket on my running pants and pulled it out. It was quite early for anyone to be calling me, even a bill collector.

"Hello," I said with confidence. Even if it was a bill collector, I could pay him off soon with my $85,000 per year.

"May I speak with Joyce Davis?" the voice on the phone asked.

"Speaking," I said, trying not to pant into the phone.

"This is Tracy Johnson, from Game Over," Tracy said.

"Oh, yes. Hello," I said, trying to hold in a girlish grin.

"Look, I apologize for calling so early. I have to catch a business flight and I'll be tied up for the remainder of the week, so I wanted to catch you before I boarded." Tracy paused to take a breath.

I took a breath at the same time.

"I really enjoyed our interview and I have a lot of respect for Charles' recommendation of you. After consideration, I would like to offer you the job," he said.

"Really?" I asked in disbelief.

"Absolutely. If you're still interested, that is?" Tracy asked with doubt in his voice.

"Well, I've recently received another offer. Would you mind giving me some time to think it over?" I asked, completely overwhelmed by the good news.

"I was hoping to get an answer today, because we need someone on board immediately," Tracy said quickly.

"I understand," I said. "Still, it's a big decision. Is it okay if I give you an answer by the end of the day?"

Tracy agreed and gave me his email address so that I could reach him once I had made a decision.

I immediately sent a text to Charles to see if he could meet for lunch. Surprisingly, he responded right away and was eager to know about my good news, which I thought I would keep under wraps until I saw him.

At work later that day, I drafted my resignation letter with great enjoyment. I typed each word with a smile, eager to see the look on my boss' face when I handed it over. The man had denied my promotions, cross training and even mere job shadowing for fear I might neglect my meager daily duties. I was going to marvel in pure joy when giving my notice.

I wrote a very nasty letter just to get my

frustrations out, but later replaced it with a more professional letter.

When I was walking out for lunch, I quietly placed my sealed letter on my boss' desk while he was on a call. I grabbed my handbag from the locked drawer in my desk and made a quick exit.

I sat in a tiny bistro in the downtown area waiting for Charles to show up. I was less worried about getting back to work on time and more elated about sharing the news with Charles.

Finally, he arrived in a hasty panic, apologizing for his tardiness. One of his meetings ran late because a project was over budget and behind schedule.

"So what's going on?" Charles asked, standing with his hand resting on the back of the chair.

"Wow, you don't waste any time do you?" I asked, joking.

His face showed his impatience.

"I got the jobs!" I squealed.

"Wait. Did you say jobs?" Charles asked with one eyebrow raised.

"Just when I thought no one wanted to hire me, I got two calls and now I don't know which offer to accept."

"Well, which offer is more appealing?" Charles asked, taking a seat.

I pulled out my new leather portfolio and extracted both offers, which I had printed out before I left for lunch. Ashli, Tracy's assistant, had sent an official letter shortly after I arrived at work.

Charles grabbed the papers and surveyed them with a deep look in his eyes.

"Good." Charles nodded as if he were a professor at the local university.

"The software company certainly pays more," I noted, "but the gaming company has lots of great benefits."

"I see," said Charles, flipping from one page to another.

"You do realize that Tracy's company offers a bonus at the end of the year?" Charles pointed out with one eyebrow raised again.

"I don't know anything about bonuses," I said shyly. "I've only heard about them in meetings where I have taken notes."

"Well, they are good things," Charles murmured as he continued to peruse the documents. "It looks like the software company will give you an opportunity to travel and really get some experience above the ground level."

At this point, Charles was more talking to himself than me and he was only repeating things I already knew. The question was which job I should take.

"This is a tough decision, considering your options," Charles said, setting the papers down on the table and crossing one leg, letting his foot dangle across the other knee.

"I know. That's the dilemma. *And* Tracy wants an answer by the end of the day," I said, pouting.

"Well, that is some news," Charles said, smiling. "The only advice I can give you is to go with the place that will make you happy and that you will enjoy going to every day. Most weeks, I work more than the typical forty hours, but I love what I do and I love my company, so it's easy for me. I'm not going to tell you to go with Tracy's company because he's my friend or with the software company because it pays the most, but think real hard about where you can see yourself five years from today."

"Those are all good points," I said, while thinking at the same time.

"You should also consider the culture," Charles continued, "and what the environment felt like during the interview. Did the employees look happy, sad or tired?"

I did not say anything, I only nodded. We both

ordered a salad for lunch and I couldn't stop talking about my two job offers. Charles suggested that moving forward, after I chose a job, we should try to meet once a month with a phone call in between, just so he wouldn't lose track of me and my progress.

As I waved goodbye, I promised to let Charles know as soon as I had made a decision.

I was still considering my new career options as I walked into the parking lot and approached Frank— which is what I named my car, after my grandad who was also old, yet dependable. He had given me the car as a gift when my last one had literally surpassed its last leg and I was in between jobs. Frank and I had seen some good and bad times, but the car was paid for and it was reliable.

My mind circled around the money I could make at the software company. I had never imagined I would be capable of making that kind of money and it would help me get out of debt and maybe one day upgrade Frank to a newer model.

I was also reaching the end of the grace period on my student loans and I needed to consider that additional bill as well.

I said a prayer as I started Frank up and he puttered. I made my way back to work, where I was eager to see the response that my boss would give to my resignation letter. It made me smile to think of the look on his face when he read the words I had typed on the page.

The only thing I would miss at that place was my close friend and colleague Cindy, who would be devastated to hear my good news. I had been so caught up in telling Charles, that I realized I had not shared the good news with Cindy.

As I pulled into the dark, underground parking garage, that I had to pay to use, I thought to myself that Cindy would have to wait. I had made a decision on what job to accept and first I needed to let my new boss know that I would be ready to start work in three weeks.

3 THE FIRST DAY

It was my first day at my new gig and I had chosen a crisp, white blouse and tan slacks. I felt refreshed and ready to get started. I decided to take a week off in between quitting my old job and starting my new one to clear my mind, meditate and refresh.

I thought I had made a good decision, because I realized I couldn't remember the last time I had a pedicure or a quality vacation. Tight budgets meant I had to give up simple luxuries.

It had been decided that I would come in around 10:00 am to avoid the morning rush. I sat in Tracy's large corner office, waiting for him to come in from a meeting. I was nervous and tried to convince my pores to refrain from releasing sweat.

"Good morning and welcome!" Tracy's deep voice boomed as he entered the office.

"Thank you," I chimed, standing as he walked

around the desk.

"Sit. Sit," he said. "You will have a busy day and I just wanted to take some time to welcome you to Game Over and let you know we are excited to have you on board. I think you will fit in really well here," Tracy smiled.

"Well, I'm certainly excited to be here and I can't wait to get started," I smiled back.

"I'm sure you remember my assistant, Ashli. She is in charge of on-boarding, so I'm going to shift you over to her so you two can get started," Tracy said, as he called Ashli into the office.

"Be sure to swing by my office around noon, because I want to take you and the other PMs to lunch for an informal introduction," Tracy said, picking up his ringing phone.

"Sure," I said as I was whisked away by Ashli.

Ashli was very thorough and had all of my tasks outlined in a handy document. She guided me through the welcome ceremony, handing me endless binders, Game Over paraphernalia and most importantly, an official Game Over badge.

For each person I met, they gifted me with what appeared to be some type of action figure. Ashli informed me that it was tradition for game developers to gift figures from games they created to newcomers.

I spent the better part of my morning being introduced to a number of people I would never remember and visiting at least a hundred break rooms. One break room was filled with comfortable-looking chairs the size of my bed, while others had recreational gaming equipment.

"Is this a company or an amusement park?" I asked, not realizing I said it out loud.

"Well, Game Over likes to make sure the employees are in a fun and healthy environment," Ashli explained with a smile.

Fun. Right. I thought again about the reason why I

had chosen Game Over; it was primarily because the software company had reminded me of my old company: drab, boring and absolutely no fun.

Ashli showed me that next to the exercise room, there was a miniature size bowling alley and a small foam room where employees could let off steam.

"Interesting," was all I said, feeling a bit out of place. Did people really let loose like that while they were at work?

It was almost noon by the time Ashli took me back to my desk so we could make a list of needed supplies. I decided to leave my collection of binders at Ashli's desk to go have lunch with Tracy and the rest of the project managers.

Tracy offered me a ride in his car and while uncomfortable at first, I slowly melted into the butter leather seats of his BMW that looked like it had been purchased the day before.

"You know I..." he started. "I didn't hire you for your experience; I hired you because you are moldable."

I sat quietly, not sure if that was a compliment or an insult.

"I want you to soak in as much as you can and learn as much as you can from the team. They are all go-getters and really brilliant individuals," Tracy went on.

I started to feel smaller, and smaller, wondering if those same butter leather seats were swallowing me whole.

I didn't respond; I only looked straight ahead, not sure what to make of the conversation.

"We have a strong mentor program, but I know that you have been working with Charles and I think you should stick with him. He's a good, strong project manager. I've tried to steal him a couple of times, but he's happy where he is at the moment."

Tracy finished his speech as we pulled into the parking lot at the restaurant. We all seemed to arrive at the same time entering the food establishment like a herd of cows going to slaughter.

I chose a seat not too far from Tracy. I didn't want to offend him by sitting too far away, but I wanted to be far enough to forgo any further speeches for the day.

As I fiddled with yet another salad, I took mental notes of the people I would be working with in my new role. My new *colleagues.* All professionally trained project managers. Tracy managed a small group, but apparently it was growing very quickly. Starting with me.

They all seemed nice, happy and friendly, except for one woman named Amber Botts. Willy didn't say much. He ate with his face close to his plate and his mouth focused on his food and not the conversation. He was definitely the oldest in the group. He was even older than Tracy, but I was not sure if he was the one who held the abundance of knowledge.

Marvin was an egotistical jokester who interjected

every serious moment with a pompous joke.

I did what I could to mingle, but I was far from the social type and found the lunch bordering on the line of discomfort.

"So where did you come from?" Marvin asked, taking a big bite of an unhealthy cheeseburger that looked nothing short of delicious.

"A very drab and boring place," I smiled.

"I think I've been there before," Leslie smiled and lifted her fork in camaraderie.

Leslie seemed content and easy to get along with and much more mature than Marvin. Amber was gorgeous and rude. She rolled her eyes, cut me off while I was talking, and I wasn't sure, but I think Amber had intentionally bumped into me when we were all entering the restaurant.

The lunch was a bit of a success and the team, for the most part seemed like a group I could work with.

***

Back at the office, I decided to forget about Amber and marvel in the fact that I had just heard Ashli say, "And this is your office."

I stood in front of an office with no window and only enough room for two small chairs and a bookshelf, as well as what would be my desk and chair. It certainly wasn't Tracy's office, but coming from a boring cubicle, this was definitely an improvement.

This would be my first office. I didn't care that it had no window and that it was small. It was my office and it had a door. It also had a frosted glass front that appeared to be see-through, but Ashli noted that it was not transparent and was mostly used as a whiteboard during meetings.

"I'll let you get settled," Ashli said as I snapped out of my daze. "Do you want the door open or shut?"

"Open. Thanks," I mumbled as Ashli almost

skipped back to her desk.

Tracy had scheduled an after lunch meeting so I could meet my project team. While I was in an entry level position, Tracy reminded me that he would not snub on the responsibility, but promised to only start me off with one project at a time.

I remembered from the interview that my group would be projectized, which meant that I would have the same team for every project I managed. The other PMs would get a new team every time a project was assigned, which meant the rest of the organization used a matrix approach.

In my old company, there were PMs for specific roles, which I gathered made them a functional structure. In my past experience, I found the functional structure very difficult for advancement. Here, I felt very lucky to have my own team and was delightfully energized at the thought of having full control.

My team was made up of four people, who all seemed quite indifferent, except for Jessica.

Jessica was a young and spicy girl who would work as my project coordinator, helping to manage metrics and provide day-to-day support. Jessica had only started one week before me so she was just as wet behind the ears.

Bruce was a big guy who seemed surly and unloved. He appeared to be very knowledgeable about the company and it was clear he didn't get out much. Bruce would be the business analyst, responsible for collecting requirements and making sure the team and the end user were on the same page. Tracy had noted that Bruce would double as a vendor manager since his role didn't last for the length of the project.

Max was the technical coordinator responsible for any technical aspects of the project, and finally, there was Rej, an attention-grabbing marketing guy who would manage the marketing features and logistics of the projects.

I smiled at my team, not sure what to say. I felt nervous and wanted to speak with Charles, but I also needed to take charge and prove to Tracy that I was capable of leading this team.

The team sat in silence, looking at me for direction, but it was only my first day. Had I bitten off more than I could chew? They all looked at me, pens in hand, ready to jot down whatever I directed.

"I am excited to be your project manager and I am excited to have you all as members of the team. I think we will all work well together if we always keep the lines of communication open and clear," I started.

The words just fell out of my mouth and I wasn't sure what would come next.

"I am very eager to get started and learn as much as I can about you the company and the project. Because today is day one for me, I think it is best that I become better acclimated with our project and I will set up a team meeting for later this week." I tried to keep it short and sweet.

Everyone sat in their chairs, appearing in a state of vegetation.

"Well. That's it for now," I said, trying not to stammer. "I will work on getting settled and we will reconvene later in the week."

No one questioned my decision. They simply gathered their things and left the small meeting room.

I asked Bruce to stay behind to debrief me on the information he had regarding the project.

As Bruce sat in one of the infamous Game Over orange chairs, he leaned back, hands crossed over his large belly. He went on to tell me he didn't know much and that I would need to speak with the business unit who submitted the project request.

"Do you have any information at all?" I prodded.

"Usually, you start with The Vault," Bruce said, staring at me like I was incompetent.

I could already conceive that Bruce would be a challenge.

"The Vault?" I asked with a questioning look.

"Yeah! The internal online system, where all the project information is housed," Bruce shared with more irritation than ease.

I was starting to feel overwhelmed, so I ended my impromptu, unsuccessful chat with Bruce and decided to head back to my office to get settled.

For the rest of the day, I was paired with Rosie, a very nice and well-seasoned perky project manager who had been with Game Over since the beginning.

Rosie entered my office with a large-sized exercise ball.

"Are you my personal trainer?" I asked, joking and nearly dead from the emotions of my long first day.

"It's good for posture," Rosie said, bending over and rolling the ball into my tight space.

"I didn't see you at lunch." I tried to make small talk and be nosey at the same time.

"I had a meeting," Rosie said, not offering any additional information.

Rosie gave me a short tutorial on Microsoft SharePoint, which I had used before in my project administrative role. She showed me where I could locate my projects in The Vault and briefly noted that most of the other PMs used a different software, outside of The Vault, to manage Agile projects.

I didn't want to get into Agile. At least not yet. I wanted to wrap my head around just regular ol' project management. Everything seemed straightforward and Rosie had not covered anything I felt to be threatening.

While Rosie and I took a break from going through processes and procedures, I reviewed my notes on the company's reporting requirements, then took a call from Charles.

"How goes it, fellow project manager?" Charles asked.

"It goes," I said, letting my fatigue creep into my voice.

"Don't sound so excited about your new job with your pay increase and excellent benefits," Charles teased.

"It's just that I really don't know where to get started," I whined. "I'm being bombarded with so much information. I've already been assigned my first project and I don't even know what it is yet, except that it's some important event the CEO wants to put on."

"The first day is always like drinking from the fire hose. It will get easier," Charles said.

Then as if the information had just entered his brain waves, he said, "Wow! The CEO?"

"Why do you sound like it's the President of the

United States?" I asked, worried.

"Because if the CEO is your sponsor, all eyes will be on you from start to finish. You can't blow this," Charles said in a more serious tone.

"Thanks for scaring me," I said. "Have I made the wrong decision? I think I'm in over my head."

"Take a deep breath. Finish getting settled and then you can worry about everything else," Charles said with a slight chuckle.

"Thanks, Charles. I don't know what I would do if I didn't have you to talk to about this stuff," I said, slumping back in my ergonomically-positioned desk chair.

"Do they use Microsoft products in your office?" Charles asked.

"Yes. I was just being trained on the SharePoint site and now I'm setting up email in Outlook. They also have something here called The Vault that they use to manage the projects. They have the coolest logo." I went off subject, talking more to myself, glaring into my computer monitor.

"Why don't you set up a meeting for closer to the end of the week with the CEO and your business analyst... You do have a BA don't you?" Charles asked, half concerned.

"Yes, of course. Bruce," I said, feverishly taking notes.

"Good! Use Bruce. He should know the company and he will know what questions to ask," Charles continued.

"The only problem is this is the first event-based project and no one is quite sure how to get started," I said.

"That's actually a good thing." Charles sounded excited. "It will give you an opportunity to mold your team and your way of doing things. If no one has ever done it before, they won't know when you're messing up." Charles laughed.

What is up with all of this molding? I thought.

Mold me, mold projects, mold teams. Is this art class?

I thanked Charles for the hundredth time and ended the call. I finished setting up my computer system because I was eager to get to work. Administrative tasks came easily to me; it was the critical thinking that I wanted to improve upon as a PM.

I started to use Microsoft Outlook in order to schedule the conference with the CEO, Blake Derby. I had to go to SharePoint and research the organizational chart to uncover his name.

I sat in a daze glaring at the blue and purple lines going through the calendar, showing Blake's unavailability. I couldn't decide if I should invite the entire team or just Bruce, the BA.

I was sure everyone would have questions, but I didn't know if having the entire team sitting in front of the CEO with notepads and pens drawn like weapons was the best idea, so I decided against it.

I found a 30-minute slot at the end of the week and I quickly grabbed it, hoping by the time I hit send, it would still be available.

Three minutes after I sent my request, I received an email confirmation from Maggie Cartwright on behalf of Blake Derby, asking that I submit an agenda for the meeting.

Oh shoot. I knew better than to send a meeting invitation without an agenda. What was I thinking? I opened a new Word document and found an agenda template. I jotted down some things I thought would be important to discuss during my first 30-minute slot with the CEO:

- What is the scope of the project?
- What is the purpose of the project?
- What is the project budget?
- What are the project goals?

· Are there any project risks?

· Are there any project assumptions?

I gazed at the list, wondering if thirty minutes would be enough time to cover all of the areas I had listed; then I realized I had forgotten the most important question.

· What is the project's primary constraint?

I looked over the list one last time. I formatted it and added some fluff to make it look pretty. I thought it looked adequate, but I sent a quick email to Charles to ask him if he would add anything. Then I followed up with a text message so that I could get back to Blake's secretary as quickly as possible.

Charles congratulated me on creating some good questions and noted that the BA would probably have some follow-up questions during the meeting. Charles recommended that because it was an event, that I should ask the CEO to walk through his vision painting a picture of his expectations.

That's a great idea! I appreciated the fact that I had a stunning mentor willing to help. Much better than the one in the past.

I sent over my completed agenda to Maggie just in time for Rosie to re-enter my office, rolling her big exercise ball.

"Do you take that thing everywhere you go?" I asked.

"Only when I have to sit," Rosie smiled, showing off a crooked front tooth.

I finished out my first work day with Rosie reviewing some sample project templates from the document repository on SharePoint. I made a note to mark the site as a favorite, along with the time tracker, quality management system and travel planner.

As I packed up my newly loaned laptop in the gifted vinyl laptop bag, I glanced around my office and thought I might bring in a plant the next day.

I hoped the IT department would clear my laptop soon because tonight would have been a good night to take work home. I knew that the more I worked on the loaner, the more time I would spend transferring information to my permanent system.

Rosie reassured me that IT was very efficient, but that it could take some time setting up a new computer, so I might not get it until the following week.

I flipped the office light switch to the off position and took a moment to revel in my new opportunity. As I closed my door, I paused and made a mental note that Bruce had not responded to my invitation to meet with the CEO.

4 THE SCOPE

The next day, I traded in my morning jog for a few more hits on the snooze button. My first day was a workout my body had never experienced and I was still recovering.

Once I made it to the office I sat at my desk pondering the many thoughts whirling through my head.

I braced myself and did a quick meditation before leaving my office to go meet with the CEO. First, I had to hunt down Bruce to confirm he was aware of the meeting, since he never replied to my invite. Game Over was a large building and Bruce, while easy to spot, wasn't easy to find.

I finally spotted him in one of the several cafeterias and asked him if he planned on attending the meeting.

"Of course," Bruce said, tearing away at a breakfast sandwich.

"You never responded to my meeting invite," I said, trying not to sound too bossy.

"I never do. If the time is open on my calendar,

then I'm there," Bruce said, wiping crumbs from his face and patting me on the back.

I didn't know what to think of the gesture. Was he being condescending or was I taking it too personal? I kept a Q-tip posted on my tack board in my office. It was a gift from Cindy, at my old job, to remind myself to quit-taking-it-personal. I was well aware that I had a habit of internalizing everything someone said or did.

Bruce and I quietly walked into Blake's office. I quickly glanced at Bruce's shirt to make sure all of his crumbs were gone. I didn't want to look like a circus act during my first meeting with the CEO of all people.

Blake's office was probably half of the top floor. It had a 180-degree view and spectacular design. It was definitely much more professional than the rest of the building but still had a playful feel.

"Thanks for taking our meeting Mr. Derby," I said, introducing myself and Bruce.

"Call me Blake," Mr. Derby said, offering a broad smile. He came from behind his desk, and motioned us toward a round table with four chairs that had a perfect view of the best bistro in town. "This project is my baby, as they say," Blake began.

I slid out my portfolio and prepared to take notes. I glanced over at Bruce, who was doing a very poor job at looking professional. I privately slid him a sheet of paper from my portfolio and loaned him my extra pen before he could ask.

"So Joyce, I hear you have just started. When I saw your name on my calendar I didn't recognize it," Blake said, crossing his legs after sitting.

"Yes. I am the new project manager that started just this week," I said, smiling and trying not to give way to my nervousness.

"What a way to start," Blake chuckled. "I'm not into that project management stuff, but I guess we can give it a go this time around."

Red flag, was all I could think as I considered how the CEO might not fully support the organizational approach. Then I remembered he was also new to the company and had been there a shorter time than my own boss.

"Well I am very excited to get started and I thought it would be best to first understand your vision before we did any planning," I said, trying to sound as if I had it all under control.

"Good idea," Blake agreed. He looked to the ceiling as if looking for thoughts to fall into his head.

We sat quietly waiting for his response. He seemed to be in the middle of some weird ritual.

"My vision," he beamed, catching both Bruce and me off guard. Bruce nearly gave way in the tiny chair he had managed to squeeze into.

Blake began to ramble about what he considered

his impeccable vision. From what I gathered, he wanted to plan a massive celebratory competition to find the next big game for Game Over.

He compared it to conventions and gaming competitions with a hint of focus group activity, and went on and on providing examples of events he attended, while making note that he wanted our event similar but nothing like them in that it had to be the first of its kind.

"Got it," I said, trying to sound enthused and on board with the vision.

"So, got any questions?" Blake asked, glaring down at his watch.

Hold on a second, bud, I thought. He spent 15 minutes of our 30-minute meeting painting an oblique picture and was already trying to escape to his next encounter.

"I have a few," I said, pulling out my agenda print-out, which we clearly were not following.

I decided to skip the question on scope since Blake was clearly not a PM guy.

"Can you tell me the primary constraint for the project?" I asked, just getting started.

"Umm." Blake pondered the question as if he was not clear on how to answer it to his own satisfaction.

I pulled from my school days and thought back to my professor's insights on how to draw information from sponsors.

"Would you say that budget, time or scope is most important in terms of execution?" I tried the question a different way.

"Well, I will spare no expense to make sure we have this thing done before our next gaming banquet, because that's where I'll make my big announcement," Blake said, as he smiled and waved his hands in the air to emphasize his epiphany.

"When is that?" I asked.

"When is it?" Blake asked me as if I was an imposter into their world of gaming.

"It's in 10 months, 20 days and 11 hours," Bruce chimed in, smiling and resting his hands on his large stomach.

Finally, he was of some use.

"A true gamer," Blake smiled.

I tried to hide my eye roll and get everyone back on track.

"Do you have a solid budget for the project?" I asked, interrupting Blake and Bruce's gaming moment.

"Let's start with about $275,000 and see where that takes us," Blake responded.

The budget sounded reasonable, but what did I know?

"Do you expect any ri—" I started before Blake cut me off.

"Well I need to prepare for my next meeting. That

should be enough to get you started." Blake's voice echoed off the wall as he rose from his seat.

"Actually, I have a few more..." My voice trailed off as I remembered Bruce.

"Bruce do you have any questions before we go?" I asked, giving Bruce a look, begging for support.

"Nope, I'm solid," Bruce said, wiggling out of his chair.

Of course, he had no questions. I was surprised he managed to speak at all. Unfortunately Bruce didn't appear to be my only problem.

As a project administrator, I spent many days chasing down sponsors on behalf of the project managers. Considering the way this meeting went, I anticipated Blake would also give me some problems in the future.

"Mr. Derby," I started.

"Call me Blake," he said, sounding like a summer tennis instructor.

"Mr.—uh, Blake, I know you are quite busy and I was wondering if there was someone else we could go to for answers when you are not available," I inquired, hoping for a concrete answer.

"Hmm, let me think about it and I'll get back to you," Blake said, picking up his phone and calling in his assistant.

That was our cue to exit with the little information he was willing to offer.

As I took the elevator down to my floor, I considered how to best share the information from the brief meeting with my team. I thought it would be best to create a charter, but I struggled with writing a scope statement that was sensible enough to capture what had been shared.

At my desk, I jotted down some thoughts on the scope. I knew the scope statement should include the project background and purpose, budget and the timeline.

I decided it was best to forego completing a long and detailed scope document but instead, concentrate on the scope statement, making sure the charter would be thorough.

As my confidence slowly increased, I began to list out my thoughts for the most accurate scope statement:

1. The purpose of this project is to create an innovative event that combines creative exploration of gaming concepts, consumer feedback and team collaboration. The event will be planned and executed within ten months so the winner can be announced at the upcoming gaming banquet. The project will be completed within a budget of $275,000.

2. The purpose of this project is to generate attention on the next phase of gaming innovation

at Game Over through the execution of a gaming creation competition that will include consumer input and collaboration overview. Planning the execution will be covered with a $275,000 budget and span a ten-month planning period.

3. The purpose of this project is to generate attention on the next phase of gaming innovation at Game Over. The project will include the planning and execution of a gaming competition that highlights innovation, collaboration and end user input. It will also include the planning and execution of a gaming banquet where the winner will be announced. The project will take place over ten months and the cost will be within a budget of $275,000 and the primary constraint is time.

"How's it going?" Tracy asked, peering his head around my open office door.

"Great," I beamed, trying to sound excited. "I met with Blake this morning on my project and I pick my laptop up from IT this afternoon so I'm moving right along."

"Sounds good," Tracy said, racing the conversation along. "Listen, I found some old traditional waterfall material collecting dust in my office and thought you could use it for your project. How's your team working out for you?"

I thought it was too soon to mention the incompetent Bruce, so I just chanted a resounding, "fine," and smiled.

"Great! Well, I will let you get back to it," Tracy said, leaving my office.

I sifted through the documents Tracy handed me and among them all, one stood out. It was a reproduction of the knowledge area mapping diagram from the PMI PMBOK.

	INITIATE	PLAN	EXECUTE	MONITOR	CLOSE
INTEGRATION	Project Charter	Develop Project Management Plan	Direct & Manage Project Execution		Close Project
SCOPE		Plan Scope/Collect Requirements			
TIME		Plan Schedule of Activities		Control Schedule	
COST		Estimate Costs/Create Budget		Control Cost	
QUALITY		Plan for Quality Assurance	Perform Quality Assurance		
HUMAN RESOURCE		Develop HR plan	Acquire Project Team / Develop Project Team		
COMMUNI-CATION		Communication Plan	Distribute Information	Report Status	Archive Documents
RISK		Risk Management Plan		Monitor and Control Risks	
PROCURE-MENT		Plan Purchases	Request Seller Response/ Select Sellers	Administer Contracts	Close Contracts
STAKE-HOLDERS	Identify Stakeholders			Control stakeholder interest	

Project Management Institute, Inc. [A Guide to the Project Management Body of Knowledge® Guide – 5th Edition]

The PMBOK guide had been a wonderful resource for me in the past and I thought it would be a good idea to take it out and review it. I needed reassurance that I was headed in the right direction.

I placed the seemingly valuable document from Tracy in a protector sheet and hung it on the wall in my office and I placed the rest of the shared information on my bookshelf.

After reviewing the knowledge map more closely, I noticed that the project charter was one of the first documents that needed to be completed. This confirmed that I was headed in the right direction.

Normally a team was necessary to help get the ball rolling on the charter, but Bruce could not be counted on and no one else on my team had any more information than I had.

I decided to create a rough draft of the charter and set-up a second meeting with Blake.

***

I managed to get on Blake's calendar for the following week and as that day arrived, I sat in the lobby on the executive floor, along with Jessica. I decided to include Jessica on the invite, since I was a horrible note taker and I thought I might as well start putting her to use.

When Bruce arrived, I immediately regretted inviting him. Bruce was completely useless. Similar to a piece of old furniture. Like the old smelly, crumb-filled recliner that had shifted around the house before being placed in the basement.

Once in Blake's office, I didn't waste any time. I handed everyone a copy of my bleak and very rough draft of a charter.

I reminded Blake that I included it with my agenda so he had time to review it before the meeting.

"Yes of course," he said, intertwining his fingers like the evil character in a movie.

"Based on my figures, I think we will be able to save some money," I smiled. I had reached out to Rej to help me with some of the event and marketing figures.

"I think you have misunderstood my vision," Blake said with his fingers still intertwined now resting on his knee.

Bruce chuckled a laugh of betrayal and I instantly shot him a glance of disappointment.

"This has to be really big!" Blake said enthusiastically.

"Yes, sir. Of course," I conceded.

"I need an event for every stage. There has to be an event for the application submission, there needs to be constant oversight of the production of the game demos, pairings with our top developers."

"Our top developers, sir?" I asked, confused.

"Sure! How else will we get those games to where we want them to be?" Blake responded, both eyebrows raised in unison.

"Of course, sir," I said, my pen scribbling much faster than Jessica's sparkling pen with fluffy madness atop of it.

"Call me Blake," he reminded me.

"How many applicants do you expect will be accepted for the demo process?" I asked, afraid of gathering any further *new* information that would change the scope of the project.

"No more than five." Blake sounded sure. "Ten tops!"

"Ten?" I said, thinking aloud how hard it might be to get ten top gaming developers to pair with applicants. I jotted down five, hoping he would forget he suggested the higher number.

"And since you're saving money, let's beef up the showcasing banquet, where we invite our top gamers from the community to vote!" Blake smiled at himself for such a wonderful idea.

"Well sir, with the new additions, I'm not sure we will have enough, but—" I was interrupted by Blake's optimism.

"I'm sure you can make it work Joyce," he said,

reaching for his ringing cell phone. "I have to take this. Moving forward, you can filter all your questions through my assistant, Maggie."

Great, I thought as Blake turned his back to us. *No more illustrious one-on-one time with the all-great CEO.*

When I returned to my desk, I decided to finalize the project charter and begin work on my remaining planning documents. The documents would be necessary for a successful kick-off meeting.

I would need my entire team's support to complete the documents, so during my weekly one-on-one with Tracy, I requested that my entire team be re-located to my floor for more effective collaboration.

"I think it's a good idea," Tracy had responded. "But they are not going to be happy," he concluded, giving me a preemptive *I told you so* look.

***

My team and I squeezed into my tiny office since

all of the conference rooms were reserved by other PMs and their teams. I was a little embarrassed because we were joined by the senior director of business development.

When I had reached out for Maggie to join on behalf of the CEO, she declined and instead recommended the CEO's right-hand man, Michael Williams.

"Sorry for the tight confinement. I'll try to make this short and sweet," I began. "I sent you all a copy of the charter which I need to get out for approval today and I need your input to make sure everything is covered."

There was complete silence, so I continued. I was surprised how comfortable I was in my management role.

"Jessica will document your questions and concerns regarding the details, but our primary focus is to get a well-shaped charter approved so we can move forward," I concluded.

I had borrowed a portable projector from one of the administrative assistants for the presentation and used it to project an image of the charter on one of my empty walls. As soon as the image appeared, I was bombarded with a host of questions.

"This is kind of short for a project charter," Max stated as it came up on the wall.

"I was thinking the same thing," Bruce chimed in, entering my office late.

"You're late Bruce," I said, curtly but trying not to appear rude in front of Michael.

"I was moving my desk. Someone required I leave my group of BAs to sit up with the sour PMs," Bruce said, chuckling.

No one else laughed, they just looked to me for a response.

Ignoring Bruce, I continued with my meeting. "As I stated, I like to keep it short and sweet and with the CEO as our sponsor as well as a constricted timeline, we need to include the important information and keep moving."

I began to go through the charter line by line following each section with an opportunity for the group to ask questions.

"Will the candidates be allowed to use our equipment?" Max asked.

"I'm not sure," I started and gave a quick glance to Michael who stood at the back of my office near the door. He had a confidence I had never been so close to outside of Thad.

"Once the candidates are selected they will be allowed access to our equipment during the second phase," Michael answered, exuding that confidence again.

Phase? Michael had triggered a new thought for me. It would probably be best to break the project out into phases, instead of events, to better manage the work.

"Max, is it possible to automate the application process instead of having an event?" I asked.

"Yes, that won't take me no time at all to develop,"

Max answered, smiling. "But who will construct the rules?"

"My assistant and I have been working on the logistics and will draft up the final rules and procedures soon. Who should I send it to?" Michael chimed in again.

I thought about it for a few seconds. I wanted to make the right decision.

"Rej will be the best person. Rej, you can use the information to begin working on your marketing push to get the word out," I said, excited to see the progress in action.

"Got it!" Rej said with a little excitement as well.

"Once the candidates are selected, who will do the artwork?" Jessica asked a good question.

All eyes looked at Michael and he chuckled a bit. He thought for a while before responding.

"Let's add some artists to the competition and shake things up a bit. The chosen candidates will get to select one of the artists from the application pool to be on their team. Those two will be paired with a top level programmer to work on the demo," Michael stated all in one breath.

"Top programmer? I thought we were pairing with top developers?" I asked, confused.

"Blake must have gotten it mixed up," Michael said, smiling, showing a perfect set of white teeth and deep dimples.

"What do they get if they win? That's what I'd wanna know." Bruce spoke sensibly for the first time.

The question caught Rej's attention and he had his pen aimed and ready to write.

"Well, that we are still working on, but most certainly the winning artist and game eventer will be offered a full-time role here at Game Over. There will be some other ancillary prizes for second and third place, of course," Michael answered, quickly catching the time on his watch.

"A job?" Jessica questioned the prize.

"Did you know, every month we receive 5,000 applications, on average, for one programmer role?"

The question hushed Jessica's doubts.

Everyone was silently jotting down every word Michael spoke and they were all on their best behavior.

"Also! The chosen artists' and gamer's created demo will become a part of our next season line-up," Michael added.

I whispered to Jessica to make sure she was capturing all of the notes and action items as the meeting progressed.

"How do they expect us to get this done in 10 months?" Max asked, sounding pessimistic.

"Our goal is to focus on what we can do and use our time wisely," I responded.

Rosie peeked her head in my office to remind me I was late for the weekly team meeting.

I dismissed my team and thanked Michael. I grabbed my project notebook and headed to the PM conference room.

Rosie was positioning herself on her exercise ball and I was sure I saw Amber roll her eyes upon my arrival.

"Now we can get started; the queen is here," Amber mumbled, but loud enough for me to hear.

"What's her problem?" I whispered as I sat next to Rosie.

"You don't know? She wanted your job, but Tracy picked you instead." Rosie smiled and swiveled on her ball to face Tracy as he began to speak.

Why would Amber take a step down? I thought.

The team meeting was interesting. Everyone went around and explained the status of their project and areas where they needed support. I was hesitant but mentioned my problems with Bruce.

"I think someone in my group has potential, but he

does not seem to add value," I said, posing my problem to the team.

"Problems in paradise already," Amber said. This time, she spoke loud enough for everyone to hear.

"Who you got?" Marvin asked.

"Bruce Holstein," I replied, hoping Marvin was gearing up to offer advice.

"Ha, he's a dinosaur. Been here since Game Over started," was all Marvin said in reply.

"If he's not performing, he will have to be replaced," Tracy said curtly.

"New girl's getting people fired already. That's a no-no," Willy said, tapping an eraser on the conference table and keenly watching it, not looking anywhere in my direction.

Tracy ignored Willy's comment and continued on with his agenda.

"Anything else?" Tracy asked, looking at me.

"Oh, yes. One more thing. I have the hardest time finding a meeting room. Any recommendations?"

"A4," Willy said.

I was surprised that he was helping me. I took a note and paid no attention to the snickers as Tracy commented, "C'mon guys," to keep the meeting moving along.

"As you can see, I will be traveling next week and then the following week I am on a much-needed vacation."

Everyone, except me, began clapping and all laughed as if it was an inside joke.

"Ok. Settle down. Settle down." Tracy laughed a little. I was still completely oblivious. "The CFO has come to me personally complaining about the ongoing invoice issues."

Members of the team moaned and groaned.

"I know. I know. I suggested that we needed a new process, she agreed and now we are tasked with the project. Congratulations!" Tracy said with a smirk.

"I think the new chick should get it," Willy said, not even considering he just used the word *chick*.

"I sure can't take on any new projects," Amber said, checking out her nail polish.

"Is this how projects are normally assigned?" I sat up straight, not sure how to respond and very scared of how Tracy would react. I was already way over my head with the one project I had.

"Do they only work on one project at a time where you come from?" Amber asked in a demeaning manner.

I ignored her and looked at Tracy as he answered my question. "Normally, they go through the Pipeline, which is an automated system for project selection; however, this is a one off. Not related to games and came directly from one of my conversations with top leadership. So? What do you think?" Tracy asked me with a wincing, pained look.

I felt the pain on his face in the bottom of my belly, but replied with a cheerful, "Of course."

"Great! It's strictly process improvement and it should be an easy one for you and your team," Tracy said before quickly moving to the next agenda item.

I zoned out for the remainder of the meeting and was not quite sure how I ended back up at my desk in front of my computer.

I thought about how the PM team seemed to interact well with one another and wanted to create the same opportunity for my team. I sent out an optional invite for a team night out for bowling.

I felt compelled to complete the project charter for the CEO project before getting started with my newly assigned project. I downloaded the saved project charter document using the document repository on the SharePoint site and got to work.

My side conversation with Michael proved

successful and he assured me the only event necessary was the showcase banquet.

I reviewed my notes from the team meeting, which I thought was very successful. I made some additional changes to the project charter and asked Jessica to glance at it for any grammatical errors.

I felt confident in the effort that I had put into the document and thought no matter how hard I tried, it would not be perfect.

Dr. A. Arrington

PROJECT CHARTER	
Project Title:	Game Over Innovation Competition
Project Sponsor:	Blake Derby
Project Manager:	Joyce Davis

Project Purpose or Justification:

The purpose of this project is to generate buzz and gain attention to Game Over's anticipated gaming lineup. The project will also increase the level of interest in joining Game Over's team of widely respected developers and artists. The project will provide an opportunity for Game Over to recruit consumer feedback throughout the entire process, immediately harnessing a quick following.

Project Description:

This project involves planning and executing a gaming innovation competition that includes the selection, production an introduction of a new game that will be added to the new lineup for Game Over. The project includes collecting applicants, selecting competitors and showcasing the work of the candidates who will ultimately be paired with artists and programmers, working to produce a demo that will be announced and showcased at Game Over's next conference.

Project Scope Statement:

The project will include three phases which covers the planning and execution of a gaming competition that highlights innovation, collaboration and end user input.

Phase I – Application submission
Phase II – Programmer & Artist pairing & Game Development
Phase III – Showcasing banquet
The project will take place over ten months and the cost will be within a budget of $250,000. The primary constraint is time.

Out of Scope:
- Planning Annual Conference
- Candidate Gaming Quality

High-level Project and Product Requirements:

- Application Process
- Selection Process
- Marketing Material
- Consumers Group
- Event Management
- Select Vendors
- Additional work space
- Top Level Programmers

Summary Budget:

Planning - $5,000
Phase I - $42,875
Phase II - $168,625
Phase III - $47,500
Close - $6,500

High Priority Initial Risks & Assumptions:

- If the timeline is not met, then the announcement cannot be made at the conference
- If there is low applicant interest there may not be enough participants for the competition
- Infiltration of the competition by Game Over competitors
- If there are other similar competitions, then application submissions could be low
- There is an assumption that community support will be accessible
- There is an assumption that programmers will be available for pairing

Summary Milestones	Due Date
Planning	Month 1
Phase I	Month 1 - 3
Phase II	Month 3 - 9
Phase III	Month 9 - 10
Closure	Month 10

Roles	Responsibilities
Project Manager: Joyce Davis	Planning, Management, Communication, Reporting, Event Management, Vendor Management
Project Coordinator: Jessica Rue	PM Support, Metrics, Communication, Schedule Review
Business Analyst: Bruce Holstein	Requirements for project and candidate teams, Liaison between client and team, vendor management support,
IT Support: Max Temple	Technical Management, Logistics support, Technical support for candidates
Marketing Coordinator: Rej Kumar	Marketing Management, Logistics support

Project Success Criteria	
Scope	Three phases that include collecting applicants, pairing competitors and showcasing game demos.
Time	10 months
Cost	$275,000
Quality	• Glitch free gaming experience • Communication within candidate team • Consistency in end-user experience • Ease of process through each phase

Conflict Resolution Process:
1: Work through conflict between parties involved
2. PM will manage arbitration for small issues between vendors, team members and applicants
3. Look for alternative solutions to resolution before proceeding to escalation path

Escalation Path for Authority Limitations:
Project Manager – PMO Director – CEO

Project Manager Signature	Sponsor or Originator Signature
Project Manager Name	Sponsor or Originator Name
Date	Date

I ended my work day by making the final changes to the charter and sending it off to both Blake and Michael for approval.

5 THE TEAM

"Amber is such a *buzz-kill*," Rej said, yelling over the noise.

"Tell me more," I smiled.

"One of the best things about being on your team is not having to ever be on her team again," Max said, taking a small sip of beer.

The team had unanimously voted against my bowling idea and instead opted for drinks after work.

I had gotten the budget for team building pre-approved by Tracy and I was hoping drinks would be covered.

They all ordered tapas, but the bulk of the orders was in the liquid department.

"I like our small team," Jessica said, sounding naïve and innocent.

"It's cool," Rej said, popping a handful of peanuts in his mouth. "So where'd you come from, Boss?"

"Please don't call me that," I answered. "I don't want to depress you with my past working experiences," is all I would say. I didn't want to say I was embarrassed that the entire world of Game Over was new to me and I had no clue what I was doing.

"She won't last long enough for anyone to care about where she's been or where she's going," Bruce said in a drunken tone.

Everyone stopped and stared at him. He was clearly out of line.

"You will never be the boss of me," Bruce said, tipping his drink and spilling beer on the floor, nearly knocking down a passing waitress.

"I think you've had enough," Max said.

"I'll say when I've had enough and since Ms. Lady is paying, I'll never have enough," Bruce said, motioning for the bartender.

I was floored and didn't know how to respond to

Bruce's actions.

"I'm the king of Game Over, not you." Bruce pointed in my direction as he stumbled from side to side.

"Bruce, why don't you let us call you a cab?" I asked as I whispered to the bartender to get a cab as quick as possible.

"Why don't you call yourself a cab, Ms. Lady?" Bruce said, getting uncomfortably close to my face.

This is not what I was expecting when I planned the team outing.

I excused myself to go to the ladies' room. My mind was clear. I had been drinking very watered down drinks all night. I wanted to participate but didn't want to embarrass myself in front of my team by getting drunk.

"Bruce is out of control," Jessica said, entering the ladies' room. "He's the major buzz-kill."

Jessica was young and it was showing. I was smart and I didn't want to get too close and cause Jessica to misinterpret our relationship. I smiled, dried my hands and left the bathroom.

When I returned to the table, more tapas had arrived and Rej was talking about his new baby and how a night out was just what he needed after diapers and bottles.

"I didn't know you were a dad," I said, surprised.

"Yep, six months and counting," Rej said.

Bruce continued to interrupt every conversation with his drunken rants. The taxi finally came and swept Bruce away so the rest of the team could enjoy the remainder of the evening.

"Glad he's gone," Max murmured, not trying to sound biased.

"I heard he's going through a tough time at work," Rej said.

"That's no excuse," Jessica added in between singing along with the music and snapping her fingers.

After Bruce left, I was able to bond and learn more about my team and their thoughts about our future work together. I tried hard not to talk about work, but let it slip that we had already been assigned a new project.

As we laughed and talked, I couldn't help but think about my problem child, Bruce. I didn't realize that he might be having problems at work, besides not liking me, but I didn't feel it should impact his ability to put forth his best effort.

***

I was working away at home in my jammies, watching my favorite recorded shows, back to back. I had not had a weekend to myself since I started working at Game Over.

It was my goal to get my planning done for both projects just in case Tracy tried to increase my workload.

My phone rang. "Hey, girl," I heard Cindy's voice on the other end of the phone.

"Hey," I replied, letting my rushed tone convey that I did not have much time to chat.

"I have some good news," Cindy said and I could practically feel her beaming through the phone.

I truly missed my friend. Charles had been my ear for the last few weeks, so I hadn't had an opportunity to share my new experiences with Cindy.

"What? You finally tracked down that actor and you guys are going on a hot date?" I joked.

"I wish," Cindy laughed. "We finally posted the project manager job in my department. I sent a copy to your email. Did you get it?"

"I'm happy where I am," I said, trying to hold the phone and search for one of my old stakeholder templates at the same time.

"Pleeease. Just apply and see what happens," Cindy begged.

"Even if I got an interview and they made me an

offer, I'm not sure I would want it." I tried to sound kind yet honest.

"Well, I have a hot date tonight and I'm not going to tell you anything about it," Cindy teased.

"You will tell me everything! I promise we will catch up soon; I'm just swamped with work right now," I said, shifting myself on my couch.

"I know. I know. I'll talk to you soon," Cindy said before hanging up.

I glanced at the PM methodology diagram that I had brought home with me. I had posted the official Project Management Plan that mapped out how my team and I would approach the project in Game Over's document repository system, along with the signed charter.

The next item up was the stakeholder register and I thought I might as well work on the communication plan at the same time.

As I started to work on the two documents, I decided I wanted input from external team members, so I sent out a few emails before I finalized the documents. I also created a standing weekly meeting for my team and me.

While I was at it, I decided to reach out to Tracy by email regarding Bruce instead of waiting until he returned from his travels. I was irate when Bruce didn't show up to the requirements meeting I set up with Michael.

When I approached Bruce after the scheduled meeting, all he said was, "You should have reminded me," and walked off.

I was amazed at the number of people who worked over the weekend. As I worked through my planning documents, I began to receive responses to my earlier emails so I was able to complete my stakeholder register before I called it a night.

***

When I was unable to find a suitable and available meeting room, I reserved the A4 conference room as Willy suggested. Sitting in A4, I realized why he was so helpful. It took me fifteen minutes just to find the colorless, dimly-lit, damp and cold dungeon.

The room looked as if it had not been used in ages. There were cobwebs in the corners of the room and enough dust to cover a small office building. There were little to no outlets and no sign of a projector. I went on a long scavenger hunt, through the building, to locate an available portable projector. As I scurried around getting things situated, I was glad that, I was smart enough to include prep time before my meetings began.

I decided it was best to focus on my meeting and deal with Willy later, as I wrapped my sweater tightly around me to ward off the cold breeze in the room.

Despite the bleak environment, I was excited to

review my documentation that I worked really hard to create.

As a project administrator, I learned that simply posting documentation was not enough. I wanted to gather feedback from my team.

STAKEHOLDER REGISTER				
Name	Position	Role	Expectations	Influence
Blake Derby	Sponsor	Provide overall support and approval.	Project completed on time, within budget and scope.	High
Michael Williams	Sr. Business Director	Provide detailed project information and act as the voice of the sponsor.	Project completed within scope based on provided information.	High
Joyce Davis	Project Manager	Manage project activities.	To be supplied with the necessary knowledge and materials to perform and meet all success criteria.	Medium
Team	Various Positions	Provide support and lead assigned activities.	To participate and engage in a successful project.	Low
End Users	Focus Group	Provide feedback and vote on candidate demos.	Feel as if input matters and is valuable to the project.	High
Candidates	Game Programmer/Developer	To produce a timely and quality gaming demo to showcase at the banquet.	To receive high quality support from the assigned programmer and credible information throughout the process.	Low
Programmers	Game Programmer	To provide high quality and timely support to assigned candidates.	Receive adequate tools to work with candidates.	High
Customer Care	Customer Support	Provide customer care support to potential candidates and end users.	Receive adequate and updated information to be able to respond quickly and efficiently.	Medium
Game Over Staff	Various Positions	Provide insight to the impacts the competition have on the work environment.	To not experience negative impacts during the course of the project.	Low
Vendors	Various Positions	Provides high quality services and/or products for the project.	Receive adequate information to perform in respective capacity.	Medium

"Are there any questions?" I asked after I walked through the stakeholder register.

"Why is our impact as a team listed as low?" Max asked.

"Because we don't mean anything," Bruce said, walking in late yet again.

"If you look at the heading, the marking is low, because it is based on your level of influence on the project. While you can make a recommendation, you don't have a lot of influence on whether or not the recommendation is accepted; however, because we are such a small team, I may be willing to change it to medium," I said, answering Max's question.

"So influence is based on what?" Rej asked.

"It is the overall influence on the project. For example, the sponsor is high because he determines the budget and he ultimately makes the decisions, just as Michael would on his behalf," I stated with confidence.

Those courses and all of my studying was starting to pay off and I was gaining more and more confidence with every meeting.

After I confirmed there were no additional questions, I moved on to the Communication Plan, which everyone found to be straightforward and intuitive.

COMMUNICATION PLAN

Communication	Purpose	Audience	Author	Communication Method/Location	Frequency
Monthly Status Meetings	To share updates with the team on progress for assigned activities; discuss issues, risks and provide updates on action items.	Project Sponsor, Project Team Members	Project Manager	Live/Virtual Conference	Weekly
Weekly Status Minutes	To keep the immediate team, senior leadership and the sponsor of the project updated on the project schedule, risks and action items.	Project Sponsor, Project Team	Project Coordinator	E-Mail/Document Repository & PM team site	Weekly
Monthly Status Reports	To keep the immediate team, senior leadership and the sponsor of the project updated on the progress and key upcoming activities.	Project Sponsor, Team Members, Executive Leadership, Vendors	Project Manager	E-Mail/Document Repository & PM team site	Monthly
Weekly Metrics	Monitor and report progress on scheduled tasks. Troubleshoot problem areas and solve or escalate issues based on project plan.	PMO Director, Project Sponsor	Project Manager/Project Coordinator	E-Mail/Document Repository & PM team site	Weekly
Project Team calendar	Provide key project dates, team schedules, vacation and training dates.	Project Community	Project Coordinator	PM Team Site	Updated as needed
Document Repository	Share all Project documents that relate to project activity and progress.	Project Team	Project Team	Game Over Internal System	Anytime
Marketing Materials	Announcements for project competition and updates on candidates and showcase promotions.	Stakeholders, VIP's, Funding and sponsor organizations, BOD's	Marketing Coordinator	Website, e-mail, letters, fliers, posters, radio announcements	Throughout the Project
Emergency Communication	Ensuring urgent information is communicated quickly and efficiently.	PMO Director, Project Sponsor, Project Team	Responsible Party	Depending on need for response.	As necessary
Engagement Survey	To document the experiences of those on-boarding and off-boarding the project throughout it's progression.	PMO Director, Project Sponsor, Project Team	Project Coordinator	E-Mail/Document Repository	As necessary
Presentations	Created to provide project information in a format for executive viewers.	PMO Director, Project Sponsor, Project Team	Project Team	Live/Virtual Conference	As necessary

"Why do we need so many different documents?" Jessica asked, jotting down action items and notes so I could send out the meeting minutes.

"These are all planning documents so that we can

initially walk through the information needed to effectively execute the project once we kick-off." I felt like I was on a roll.

"When is our kick-off?" Bruce asked.

Finally, he is sounding interested, I thought.

"I'm hoping to schedule it for next week, since I'm almost done with the planning documents. It's a long meeting and it's tough to get on the sponsor's sched—"

"Good! You'll have the meeting while I'm on vacation," Bruce spoke over me. "I hate those things."

I had had enough. After I adjourned the meeting, I asked Bruce to stay behind so I could speak to him about his recent behavior. During my research over the weekend, I learned I would first have to give Bruce both verbal and written warnings before I could take any real action.

"Bruce, I think it is imperative we discuss your behavior because I don't think it is beneficial to the team dynamic," I started.

"Soooo, are you saying I can't take a vacation?" Bruce asked, leaning forward in a threatening manner.

"No. What I'm saying is that if you want to take a vacation, you will need to go through the proper channels and request it just like everyone else," I tried to state with a firm look.

"Hmph," was all Bruce could muster.

"I am officially giving you a verbal warning," I stated.

"Me? A verbal warning?" Bruce began to yell.

At the same moment, Willy stuck his head in the meeting room like he was attracted to the scent of fury. When he realized who it was, he quickly bypassed me to speak to Bruce.

"Hey, you ole' rascal, what you been up to?" Willy asked, ignoring the fact that we were in a meeting, even if it was an informal one.

"Babysitting," Bruce said, looking at me.

Willy glanced at me as he sat on the edge of the conference room table.

"Can't be that bad; she has the easy projects," Willy chuckled.

I had been insulted enough. I gathered my things and went to see if Tracy was available. When I got to his office, I remembered he was out.

"Dang it!" I said aloud.

I decided it would be a good idea to see if Charles was available.

"What's up, PM?" Charles answered his cell phone.

"Thank God!" I released a sigh of relief to hear his voice.

"What's going on? I only have five minutes before my next meeting," Charles replied.

"It's Bruce! It's always Bruce. He's the thorn in my side," I said, trying to get it all out in one breath.

"Did you talk to Tracy about it?" Charles asked.

"Briefly during our last one-on-one and I sent him an email this weekend, but now I'm starting to feel threatened," I said.

"Wow! It's that bad?" Charles asked.

I was close to tears and didn't answer for fear of having a breakdown at my desk.

"Well, if you feel threatened and you were my employee, I would recommend you go to HR and report the incident. As far as Bruce as a resource, I think you may have to make an example out of him, but at the same time empower the rest of your team, to show them you respect hard workers."

I was quiet, but I was still listening. Something Charles said stuck with me and I wrote it on my whiteboard to be reminded. Just as I was hanging up, I saw a call coming in from Tracy on my cell phone.

I apologized for bugging Tracy during his travels, but explained the problems I was having with Bruce.

"I'm sorry to hear Bruce isn't working out," Tracy said. I could hear the noise of the airport terminal in the background.

"I gave him a verbal warning today, but I'm not sure I can last through a written warning as well," I confided in Tracy.

"Joyce, I want to apologize," Tracy said, not truly sounding sympathetically sorry but regrettably sorry.

"What for?" I asked.

"I had no idea this project would be of this magnitude. I was under the impression the project would be small and quick. Something on your level. Are you sure you can handle it?" Tracy asked, looking for reassurance.

"I'm certainly up for the challenge. I know I can do this," I said, trying to convince Tracy, "but I need a quality team and Bruce just isn't giving me what I need."

"Okay. Let me make some phone calls and see what I can do," Tracy said.

I ended the call wishing Tracy a safe trip and telling him that I appreciated his support. I was ready to get started on preparing my schedule and budget; collecting the requirements were a huge part of making that happen. Without a good BA, I wouldn't have quality requirements.

"You might need to lighten up a little." Willy walked into my office without knocking.

"Excuse me?" I said sitting up in my chair.

"Some people have been here way longer than you and know a lot more about gaming. You're still wet behind the ears young lady," Willy said, speaking to me as if he were my father. "Bruce is a good guy and from what I hear, you're giving him a hard time," Willy went on.

"I appreciate your concern, Willy, but I can handle my own team." I tried not to sound rude to my own PM teammate.

"I've been doing this a long time and I'm only

trying to help." Willy kept on talking.

"Give it to her, Big Will," Bruce said, walking by my office and flashing a grin of victory.

"Just remember that people weren't begging to be on your team. Some people were forced and had their whole world turned upside down," Willy said as he left my office and joined Bruce in his cubicle.

I didn't know what to say or to think. I never considered how Tracy constructed the members of my team. I always thought our smaller team with less work was a privilege, but maybe I was wrong. Obviously, not everyone felt the same as I did.

I pinged Rosie on the internal messaging system to see if she could provide some answers.

> Rosie? U there?
> -Hi Newbie! What's up?
> Nothing much. I had a quick question.
> -Talk to me...

Do you know the back story on Bruce?

-Hmm not really. Think he was cross training before

going to your team. Been working here for ages.

Moved around a bit.

Do you know why?

-Nope!

Thx!

-Np...

At that moment, I decided to have monthly one-

offs with my team so they could discuss highs, lows and

opportunities for growth. I also thought it was the perfect

opportunity to draft my Human Resource Plan for my

project.

I scanned my HR Plan for errors, incorporated

some of Game Over's policies and procedures and made

sure each section was accurate before posting it and

sharing it on the team site.

Just as I was preparing to move on to my next task, I

received a visitor.

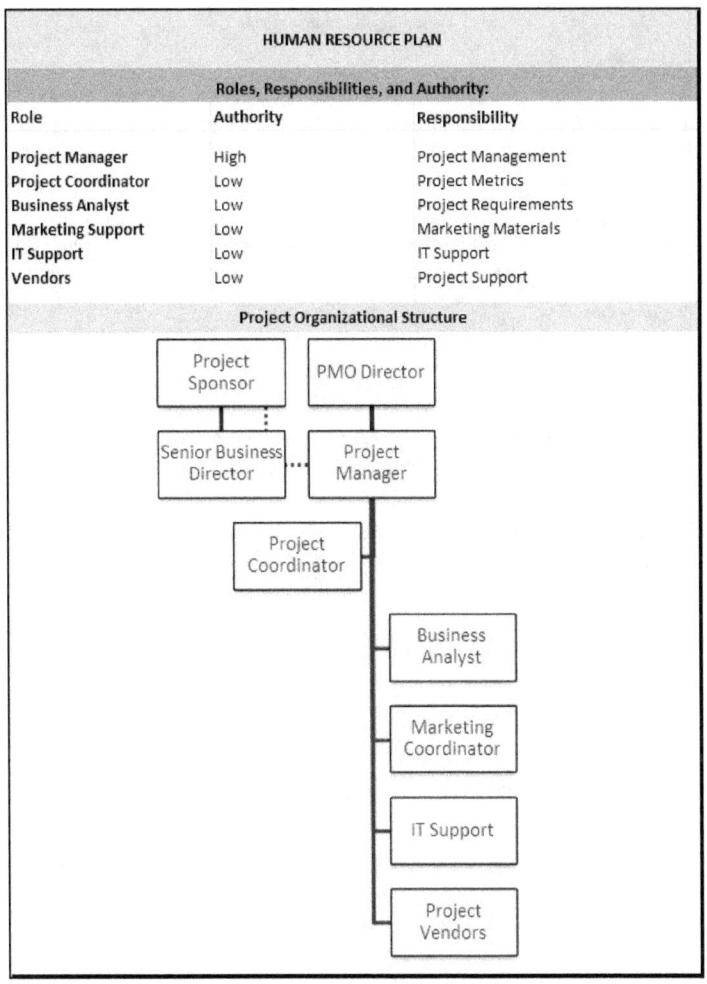

HUMAN RESOURCE PLAN

Roles, Responsibilities, and Authority:

Role	Authority	Responsibility
Project Manager	High	Project Management
Project Coordinator	Low	Project Metrics
Business Analyst	Low	Project Requirements
Marketing Support	Low	Marketing Materials
IT Support	Low	IT Support
Vendors	Low	Project Support

Project Organizational Structure

Project Sponsor

PMO Director

Senior Business Director

Project Manager

Project Coordinator

Business Analyst

Marketing Coordinator

IT Support

Project Vendors

Staffing Management Plan
Resource Acquisition
Staff will be acquired through the Game Over process of working with HR to design and post appropriate job descriptions. Candidates will be interviewed and when hired provided with the proper on-boarding experience.
Resource Release
Staff will be provided with a verbal warning, followed by a written warning and will be terminated if behavior persist. All staff, whether terminated or those who leave voluntarily, will receive an exit review.
Resource Calendars
Calendars will be kept on the Project Team website and will be updated weekly by the Project coordinator.
Vendor Resources
Vendors will be treated with high regard and respect. They will be included in status meetings and provided access to view the project documents and add insight where they feel necessary.
Training Needs
Resources will be asked to submit training requests 30 days prior to the training period. Additional training opportunities will be discussed during employee development sessions.
Rewards and Recognition
Resources will recognized verbally and through the Game Over employee recognition program for their noted achievements.

"Hi. Joyce?" A voice called from outside of my office door.

"Yes. I'm in here." I wondered who it could be now.

"Hi! I'm Laraine from HR." A pretty girl with long, curly hair entered my office.

"Hi, I'm Joyce." I stood up to shake her hand.

"Tracy gave me a call and asked me to work with

you on writing a job description for a BA," Laraine said with a smile. "He said it was urgent."

Wow, I thought, *Tracy didn't waste time and he was right, it is urgent.*

"Is now a good time for you?" Laraine asked.

"Absolutely!" I said, getting up to close my office door.

Laraine and I spent the better part of an hour drafting the perfect job description. Laraine explained that she would fully vet the sources before submitting their resumes to me for review.

I couldn't believe I would actually be responsible for hiring someone. I would be on the other side of the table.

"What will happen to Bruce?" I asked, feeling a little bit sorry for the guy.

"For now, he'll hang out with you until we can move him someplace else in the company," Laraine replied.

"Plus, we have to find his replacement."

I moaned and tried not to behave like a toddler when I heard the bad news.

"How soon can we post the job?" I joked.

"Once my manager and Tracy approves it, I'll have it posted right away," Laraine smiled. "If you want, we have a pool of BA resumes that I can forward to you and you can start looking through them while you wait."

"Perfect," I said, even though I didn't have the time to do any of it. *Another weekend working at home,* I thought.

I thought it was a good idea to walk around to check on everyone to see how they were progressing with their initial research and discovery.

I even asked about their personal lives, family and pets. I wanted them to know that I cared and I didn't simply consider them work mules. They were people. They were my team.

6   THE PLANS

I was having drinks with Charles at a nearby Happy Hour spot. It was seven o'clock and I had just left work.

"Gin dry," Charles said blankly to the waitress taking our order.

I had very little energy in my voice, as I ordered my drink and watched a bearded guy on stage tune his guitar.

"Rough day?" Charles joked as he took a quick sip of his drink.

"Rough day. Rough week. Rough project," I whined as I began to unload.

"Get rid of the BA yet?" Charles asked with a sympathetic smile.

"Yes!" I said, lifting my glass for a cheers.

"Tell me all about," Charles said, smiling.

As I stared at him, I thought he was starting to look attractive, but I quickly blamed it on my lack of sleep.

"I've been staying late every night and taking work home, trying to work through this planning material," I complained. "On top of it all, I think my team hates me."

"Remember what I told you," Charles said.

"I know, I know," I started. "*Empower them,*" we both finished at the same time.

"What stage of team development are you in?" Charles inquired.

"Somewhere around storming. Although I think Bruce started in storming and isn't moving," I laughed.

Charles joined in the laughter and reassured me that what I thought was hate was most likely fear and contempt for change.

"You're probably right. I might be overreacting," I said, taking more than one swig of my drink.

"Well, at least your bottleneck is gone," Charles said, looking at the menu.

"You are so right. You should have seen the look

on the team's face when I introduced the new BA. She's amazing. She hit the ground running," I said, smiling. "It's like we see eye to eye. She is the complete opposite of Bruce, who no one else saw as a problem."

"Well, you know perception is 80% reality and what people perceive becomes their truth. What I mean by this is that everyone has devises their own truth based on how they interpret their own individual perceptions."

"Well, the *truth* is I'm finally ready for my kick-off."

"Look at you!" Charles said in support. "Ready for your very first kick-off."

"Stop teasing!" I grinned in a flirty way. "It's been harder than I ever could have imagined. I didn't give PMs enough credit. So how's life treating you? I never get to ask how *you're* doing?"

"Oh, I'm good. Got my promotion, which means I'll have less time for you." He raised his glass again.

I reluctantly gave Charles a hearty smile and clinked his glass. He was promoted to PMO manager, which meant he would have a lot more responsibility and a lot less time for me, as he noted.

***

My team and I were meeting to review our project schedule in detail. It was going to take some time, so I had a bucketful of candy and multiple scheduled breaks.

My goal was to finalize my planning documents and schedule the kick-off meeting as soon as possible.

"Okay, as we work through the project schedule, I want you to remember that article I sent you guys on playing the estimate games." I started my meeting with high energy.

The estimate game was a hypothetical explanation for finding ways to require more time on a task than necessary. I wanted to make sure my team was completely honest about the time needed for each task.

"That article was very interesting," Nancy, the new BA, started. She was still trying to impress me. I had decided to hire outside of the company and give Bruce back to the BA department. Gladly.

"I think we should double up," Rej said, laughing.

"Yes, but if we double up, it needs to reflect in the budget and then we'll be over budget," I reminded Rej and the rest of the team.

"Just ask for more money," Matt suggested as if it were that easy.

I chuckled as I thanked Michael for joining the meeting. As usual, he would not be available to stay for the entire meeting so I decided to start with his section first.

"I already have a pretty good project shell. I need for you all to help me with duration, dependencies and keep an eye out to see if I missed anything." I pulled up the schedule on the conference room's large projection screen.

"Glad we finally got a real conference room."

Jessica said what they were all thinking.

"I think I'll need two weeks for all of my tasks," Michael confirmed as I walked through the project schedule.

"Is it possible for some to run concurrently?" I asked. "With so much policy to build, it could hurt our schedule."

Michael took a long look at the tasks and started to offer insight into where items could be connected.

"Oh no. I'm on vacation during the week you want me to select the committee. I'll try to work on it early and pass the information over to Maggie." Michael quickly offered a solution.

"Why are we preparing for pairing during Phase 1?" Matt asked.

"We need to get the programmers on board early so they are not broadsided by the demands of this competition," Michael answered for me.

He could speak for me anytime. He was smart and very handsome. And very married—lucky girl.

"Michael, how long should we allow for application submissions?" I tried to exhibit perfect posture and sound professional.

"I say three months is good."

"That's going to be tough with our timeline. Can we do one month?" I tried to slyly negotiate.

We settled on one month for acceptance of submission which gave the selection committee additional voting time.

As we worked through the schedule line by line, Michael eventually quietly exited the room to go off to bigger responsibilities.

"I'm going to need some help with the voting automation," Matt stated when we reached a section of the plan that reflected his work.

"Which automation?" I asked to confirm if he

meant voting for the competition candidates or for voting during the banquet.

"Both. I won't have the time, nor do I have the knowledge to put it together myself, but I'm sure I can find someone who can," Matt said, flipping his pen around on the table.

"I thought you said it would be easy," I reminded him.

"I was wrong."

"Rej, will you also need to outsource some work?" I interrupted Rej who was glancing at his phone.

"Probably," he said, looking up.

"I want you to note areas where we can save money. For example, there may be things we can outsource so we don't have so much pressure on our team," I said, taking Charles' advice to empower the team. "We should identify outsourcing needs as soon as possible because I would like to invite the vendors or contractors to join our kick-off meeting."

Keeping the schedule within the 10-month constraint would be difficult. Most of the time would be allotted to the game demo creation and everything else should be condensed.

I used the moment to gather feedback from the team. We made a decision to outsource the voting automation, promotion printing, and event logistics, just to keep things simple.

While I had created phases for the project schedule to make the information easier to follow, the team still had questions.

"Why is my name down for documenting the process for the demo development?" Matt sounded disappointed.

"I will be loaning you and Nancy to the competition. During the period you are working with the candidate teams, your workload with our team will be extremely low," I said, trying to re-build Matt's engagement.

Nancy simply nodded her head. She was happy to be on board and did pretty much whatever I asked.

"I will need at least double the time," Matt stated with an attitude. "I will be working with five different teams. That's quite a lot."

"I don't mind adding a little buffer for you, Matt, but we cannot double time for the sake of doubling," I said firmly. "The work will be staggered and I will have you review Jessica's calendar before it's published."

The mere mention of Jessica's name always caused her to ask random questions.

"Why do you have roles listed instead of names and why is the programmer responsible for all of the game demo work?" Jessica asked, trying to soak in as much as she could.

"It's important to have, in a figure of speech, a

throat to choke. If I need information, I should be able to go to the programmers and not have to reach out to the candidates and artists. This would essentially hold them responsible for their team. As for naming, it makes it easier in the event there are more changes in the team." I smiled a teasing, yet threatening smile.

"Ok," I continued enthusiastically. "Good work team! Once I have the results of your research on your needed vendors, I can use that information to complete the budget. Rej and Matt you will need to let me know your decisions so I can get started on the Statement of Work." I was so ready to end my very long meeting.

I had taken over vendor management when Bruce was removed from the team and I didn't want to hand over the responsibility to Nancy, who was newer than me.

"Got it," they both confirmed at the same time.

"As usual, Jessica will send out the action items in an email and add them to our team site. Also, please do not forget to pass your holiday and vacation time to Jessica so I can keep the calendar updated." I yelled the final sentence as my team hurried from the conference room to get started with the load of work they acquired during the meeting.

I remained in the conference room alone and continued to work on the plan. I added lag time to some tasks to cover additional buffers of time later on when I knew development might snag.

I simultaneously worked on my budget, adding hours for the resources based on the time calculated in the project schedule.

"I need to kick you out," Tracy said, coming into the conference room with a group of people.

I had overstayed my time and needed a walking break anyway. Sometimes I left the building to walk the beautiful campus or just take a seat on one of the benches outside.

"Did you finish the charter for the process project?" Tracy asked, setting up his laptop.

"Yes, I did. It's in the cloud," I said, smiling and packing up my things.

As I left the conference room, I dropped my things in my office and headed down to the free cafeteria to grab a green tea and muffin.

I ran into Bruce on my way out, who gave me a snarl. I just smiled and sipped my tea, glad to be free of that headache.

"Hey! Joyce right?" a guy asked, sitting next to me on the bench.

"Yes," I said, showing off my radiant smile and white teeth.

"I'm Jonathan and I heard about your project. The competition. That's your project, right?" he asked.

"Yes," I answered, trying to figure out where the conversation was going.

"Well, I'm a new programmer. I've only been here a few months but I would love to be in the competition," Jonathan said.

"You mean you want to be on the pairing list?" I asked, surprised. My team and I thought one of the hardest things would be pulling the programmers from their work.

"No. I have a great idea I want to enter." Jonathan's eyes lit up.

My team and I had never considered that current employees might want to compete.

"Oh," I said, my mind racing to give him a sufficient answer without alienating myself from yet another co-worker. "Unfortunately, the competition is for non-Game Over employees. You see, the prize is a job with the company; but I can put you on the list to be considered for the pairing," I explained.

"Oh." Jonathan sounded and looked disappointed.

"Ok. Thanks."

Jonathan left as quickly as he appeared and I finished my tea. I thought about how I could make my kick-off meeting different from those I attended in the past. They were always so boring, drab and long.

I had time to think about it and would continue to work through some ideas in my head. On my way up to my office, I met Blake in the elevator.

"How's the project?" Blake asked. "I hear it's going smoothly."

"Yes, it is," I said, thinking if I had any questions for him. "So far, so good. The budget is right at your proposed limit."

"But not over?" Blake inquired.

"No, not over, but I was wondering if I could get a 10% contingency for the risk plan?" I tried to slide that one in.

"Risks?" But I thought you said everything was

fine." Blake looked worried.

"Well everything is fine now, sir, but there are always things that come up that we don't know about." I tried to soothe his concern.

We quickly passed my floor but I stayed on the elevator to see if I could get the contingency approved. Blake reluctantly agreed.

"Hey! I was thinking we could have someone perform at the banquet. You can use what's left in the budget," Blake smiled as he exited the small space and the elevator doors closed.

Perfect. Blake was already making more changes before the project had even officially started. I remembered that there was something I could do to help manage it. I went to find Rosie.

"Hey, Rosie! What's that thing called where it stops people from making changes to your project?" I asked in a rush.

"I don't know, but if you find it, you can make a lot of money off it," Rosie joked.

"You know what I mean. It's a process of some sort." I tried to be serious.

"Oh, you mean Change Control," Rosie reminded me.

"Yes! Change Control. Do we have that here?"

"We do, but it's different for our Agile projects. You will have to most likely create a process for your projects. Tracy should be able to help you with that. I'm swamped," she said, patting me on the shoulder and heading into a conference room.

"New girl needs help again," Amber said, walking by and rolling her eyes.

I was surprised they were still in her head as much as she rolled them.

When I returned to my office, I sent a quick email to Charles to see if he could share a template for a Change

Control plan.

***

I was meeting with my team to go over the final review of the risks. The list was long and I wanted to work out the numbers so that they could focus on the high risks.

We started off the process by creating thresholds for what was important, setting a 10-point scale for impact and a 100% scale for probability. This would make it easier to rank the risks.

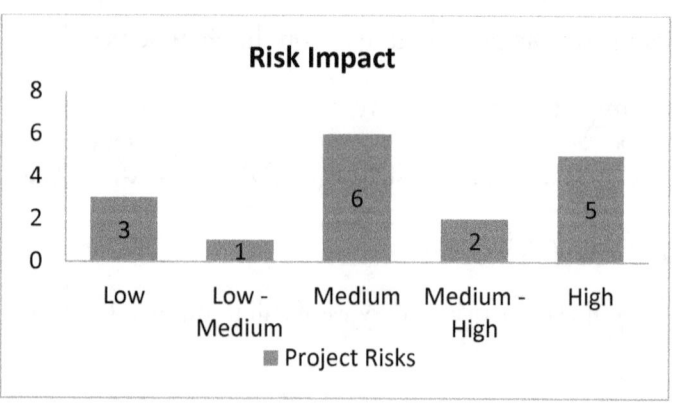

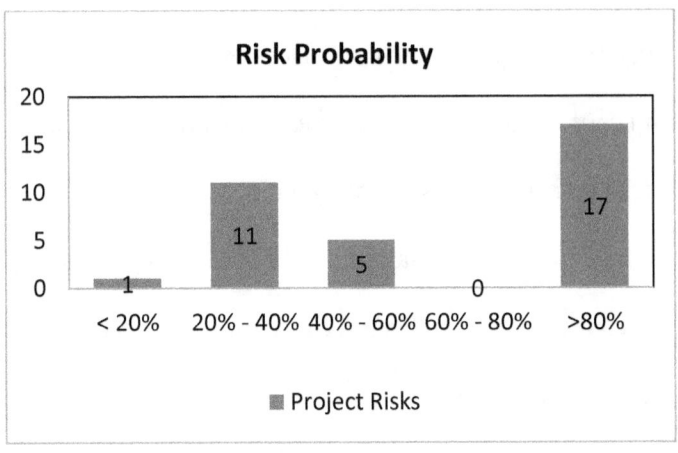

"Currently, we are looking good. We have a lot of low probability, but high impact. This means if you own a risk, you have to keep your eye out for triggers," I said, reviewing the final numbers.

"What are triggers?" Rej asked, looking tired. The new baby must have had him up late.

"We want to keep our eye out on triggers and symptoms. For example, if you have a cough, it's usually a symptom of a cold, so you know you must act before it gets worse. If someone who was sick coughed on you, perhaps it triggered you getting the virus. Does that make sense or am I confusing everyone?" I asked, remembering some notes I reviewed on risk management.

"No, I get it," Max said. "We are looking for things that could happen that could cause the risk to occur and if it does, we have to put our plan into action."

"Exactly." I was excited to be making sense.

Risk Identifier	Risk & Impact	Probability				Strategy/Response	Costs	Assigned To
Phase I								
R.100	Information Management: if there is a loss of data in the PM system, the project will lose planning time.	30%	7		2	**Mitigate:** Secure Backup of project information using the cloud system.	$45	Project Coordinator
R.101	Information Management: Internal theft and sharing with competitor could impact the participation level of the project.	30%	5			**Mitigate:** Place strong restrictions on data access and track which resources are accessing information.	$45	Project Coordinator
R.102	Human Resources: Complaints filed by staff could impact the morale of the team engagement.	30%	7		2	**Mitigate:** Provide a working environment and communication path that allows the PM to first work through issues before complaints are filed.	$45	Project Manager
R.107	Human Resources: Immediate team members need to be replaced in and their work needs to be reassigned.	10%	7			**Accept:** Quickly work to get new resources on boarded and make sure previous resource properly documents status and previous work completed.	$25	Project Manager
R.113	Competition: There are too many applicants to review in the time period provided.	30%	3			**Exploit:** Use it as a publicity notion and exploit the opportunity to threaten cut off time due to applicant overload.	$75	Senior Business Director
R.114	Competition: The application pool is low, impacting the number of quality applicants from which to choose.	40%	9		4	**Accept:** Provide additional time to collect more applications and institute a harder marketing push for promotion.	$240	Marketing Coordinator
R.121	Estimates: Team provides inadequate estimates for work impacting schedule and budget.	40%	9		4	**Avoid:** Provide resources with a platform to be comfortable with providing accurate depictions of work durations.	$100	Project Manager
R.126	Judging: Judges have a conflict of interest in voting for final candidate list, which impacts the ability to move forward.	40%	8		3	**Mitigate:** Create a process that provides a resolution for deadlock in voting activity.	$240	Marketing Coordinator
Phase II								
R.133	Procurement Issues: if Vendors do not provide quality service for the project, it could impact the schedule and overall quality of the project.	20%	8		2	**Mitigate:** Create a clause in the contract that protects our project from receiving lower quality than promised.	$90	Project Manager
R.149	Technology Issues: Application submission system crashes and potential candidates are not allowed to submit their application.	25%	9		2	**Mitigate:** Conduct daily checks on the health of the system and include a "report" button if a user needs to report an issue.	$125	IT Coordinator
R.155	Resources: Candidates leave the competition decreasing the number of total participants.	25%	7		2	**Mitigate:** Provide programmers with tools to keep team members motivated and engaged throughout the process.	$125	Programmer
R.167	Schedule: Team not meeting deadline which impacts the ability to meet the conference date.	30%	9		3	**Avoid:** Remain in constant communication with Programmer leading the team to ensure proper resources and material are provided so team can meet given deadlines.	$1,500	Project Manager
R.172	Resources: Programmer needs to be replaced due to workload conflicts. This will impact the ability of the candidate to complete their work.	50%	7		4	**Mitigate:** Create opportunities for stand-by programmers to stay abreast of project progression in the case they are needed.	$250	IT Coordinator
Phase III								
R.174	Event: Event staff performs a poor job during the event causing a poor experience.	20%	4		1	**Transfer** Risk to Event Company. Provide alternative event staff if the need arises.	$100	Event Contractor
R.189	Event: Equipment Failure. This could create a negative reputation for the ability of the company to create solid events.	40%	3		1	**Transfer** Risk to Event Company. Conduct onsite walk through to ensure the material is functioning properly. If any issues are noted, refer them to the Event Company	$200	Project Manager
R.194	Quality Management: Food and beverages are not as promised could impact the level of ambiance created for the event.	30%	7		2	**Mitigate:** Confirm catering menu has been tested and approved prior to selection being prepared.	$375	Culinary Arts
R.200	Quality Management: Logistics. The sound and lighting are not working and create a delay in the program.	20%	9		2	**Transfer** Risk to Event Company. Conduct onsite walk through to ensure the material is functioning properly. If any issues are noted, refer them to the Event Company.	$250	Project Manager

Everyone scanned the Risk Register to see if they had any last minute comments or questions. There were originally over 100 risks, but we managed to scale it back and focus on those we thought were most important.

"We will review this weekly because sometimes risk levels can change as the project progresses," I said. "We will be able to quickly identify the high-level risks by the identifier in the ranking column. I have them color-coded based on low, medium and high risks.

"I almost forgot, Rej. We now need to look for a banquet headliner," I said, smirking.

The statement made Rej look even more tired than he appeared.

"I've already added it to the schedule and Jessica can help you with your research." I tried to remove some of the pressure. "I've also created a solid change management process that should hopefully control the number of changes we receive in the future."

Once the meeting was finished, I had finally completed all of my planning documents. Unfortunately, Rej and Max moved slower than I expected, so I had to push my kick-off meeting out further. I was wondering if I should question their estimates in the schedule.

I was able to use some downloaded templates to create what I thought was a great presentation. I wanted to use Prezi, but thought with common technical issues in the only conference room I could book, it was best to stick with PowerPoint.

I sent out my agenda and expected the entire team and my vendors to be on board. The agenda made for a long meeting, but provided a quick review of each of the major sections I found to be important.

Time	Agenda	Speaker
10:00 AM	Welcome/Introduction	ALL
10:15 AM	Set Project Expectations	SPONSOR
10:30 AM	Review Project Charter	PROJECT MANAGER
10:45 AM	Review Project Scope	SPONSOR
11:00 PM	Review Project Schedule	PROJECT MANAGER
12:00 PM	Break/Lunch	ALL
12:30 PM	Review Project High Risks	PROJECT MANAGER
1:00 PM	Review Communication Plan	PROJECT MANAGER
1:15 PM	Review Change Control Process	PROJECT MANAGER
1:30 PM	Review Project Budget	PROJECT MANAGER
1:45 PM	Discuss Vendor responsibilities and interaction.	PROJECT MANAGER/VENDORS
2:00 PM	Discuss Next Steps	SPONSOR
2:15 PM	Review Action Items	PROJECT COORDINATOR
2:30 PM	Feedback/Questions	ALL
2:45 PM	Adjourn	PROJECT MANAGER

Because my meeting was early and would run long, I had arranged for Jessica to bring continental breakfast items for the morning session and sandwiches during the lunch break for those attending in person.

I remembered being in Jessica's shoes and tried to treat her with respect while also giving her a chance to shadow and learn. I hoped she was up for the challenge.

7 THE KICK-OFF

I was in my one-on-one with Tracy, feeling very nervous about my upcoming kick-off meeting. I had planned my kick-off to follow my one-on-one meeting with hopes my nerves wouldn't be frazzled.

I used my time with Tracy to review my Change Control process. I was able to use the template Charles sent me which was strangely simple. I made a few adjustments since I didn't have a Change Control Board and asked Jessica to create an online change submission form and log.

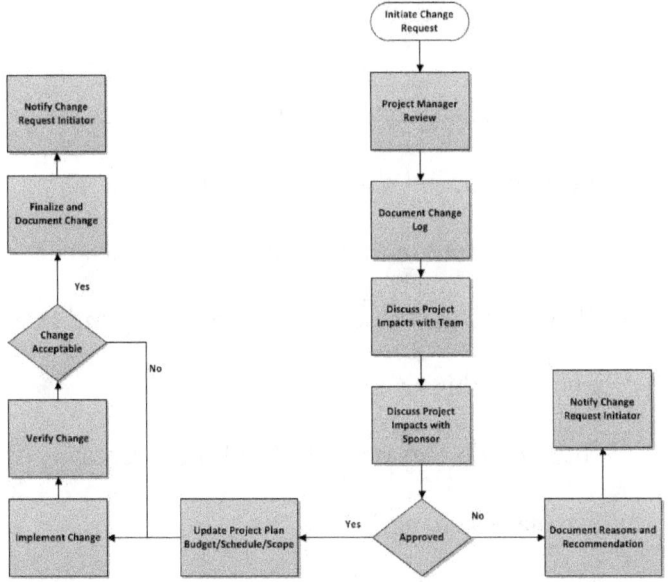

"Looks good to me," Tracy said, handing me my document.

"That's it? No other comments?" I asked, wanting more feedback.

"Have you set your freeze date?" Tracy asked, grabbing a power bar from his top drawer.

"My what?" I looked completely confused. I was so tired, I no longer cared about looking or sounding confused.

Tracy laughed a bit. "Your freeze date. The date you will no longer accept changes for the project."

"I can have one of those?" I asked in amazement.

They didn't use those at my old company and I was quite glad to hear this news.

"But how do I say no to the CEO of the company if he wants to make a change?"

"I know it's difficult, but you first have to get him to sign off on the date and then get his support on enforcing that date," Tracy smiled.

"Great. It's not as good as it sounds." My posture changed.

Tracy glanced at his watch to signal the meeting was going over the allotted time.

"The key is to make sure Blake follows the rules, then everyone else will follow his lead."

"Got it," I said. But I didn't really get it. It sounded

a lot easier than it probably was.

I left Tracy's office and considered the new information he provided. I wasn't completely convinced that a scope freeze date would work with Blake, but I was willing to give it a try.

I was still nervous and a little shaky as I double-checked with Jessica to ensure everything was all set for the kick-off meeting. I probably needed a sedative more than anything, but decided to put on my big girl pants and get it done.

I would be sure to keep my eye out for people falling asleep. My team and I had already seen the information I would be covering, so the meeting would most likely benefit the vendors and Blake.

I had planned a few interactive activities throughout the meeting just to keep people on their toes. I arranged for moments during document review where they could be engaged by providing feedback.

I began the meeting with introductions and a quick ice breaker to loosen up the group.

After covering the objectives of the project, I used a WBS to share a very high-level view of the project. I thought it would make it easier to walk through the actual project schedule in detail.

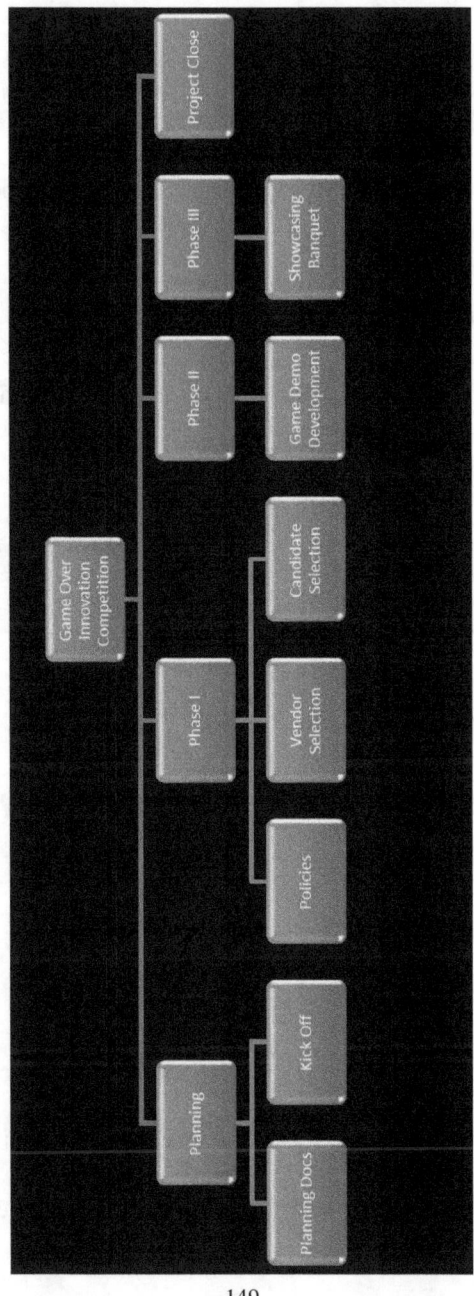

Next, I took my time working through each section of the detailed project schedule, starting with dates, so deadlines and expectations were made clear for both the vendors and my team.

Project schedules could be hard to follow for those outside of project management and I wanted to ensure everyone understood the document.

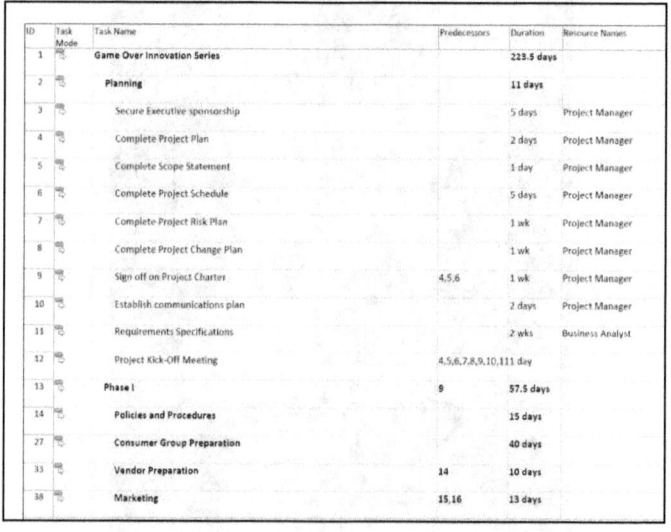

ID	Task Mode	Task Name	Predecessors	Duration	Resource Names
1		**Game Over Innovation Series**		223.5 days	
2		**Planning**		11 days	
3		Secure Executive sponsorship		5 days	Project Manager
4		Complete Project Plan		2 days	Project Manager
5		Complete Scope Statement		1 day	Project Manager
6		Complete Project Schedule		5 days	Project Manager
7		Complete Project Risk Plan		1 wk	Project Manager
8		Complete Project Change Plan		1 wk	Project Manager
9		Sign off on Project Charter	4,5,6	1 wk	Project Manager
10		Establish communications plan		2 days	Project Manager
11		Requirements Specifications		2 wks	Business Analyst
12		Project Kick-Off Meeting	4,5,6,7,8,9,10,11	1 day	
13		**Phase I**	9	57.5 days	
14		**Policies and Procedures**		15 days	
27		**Consumer Group Preparation**		40 days	
33		**Vendor Preparation**	14	10 days	
38		**Marketing**	15,16	13 days	

"Will we have access to your project schedule?" the venue representative asked during the Phase III review.

"You will not have access to our system, but each week I will send you an updated pdf so you can be informed of our progress," I responded.

"Currently, our programmers are working in Agile and I'm not sure they will be able to follow this process as well," Michael said, concerned.

He was very affluent in project management and was adding some great value to the meeting.

"This is a one-off project and I have a process in place where Jessica will work with them to build a calendar," I stated.

"It sounds like double work to me," Michael said, not convinced.

I really wanted to impress Michael and I wasn't sure what else to say.

"We will do our best to keep them on track," I said with a smile.

"What's a go/no go?" Nancy, the new BA asked,

unfamiliar with the term. "I saw it more than once throughout the schedule."

"These are presentations that are conducted in the PM process that help determine if the project should continue forward or if it should be terminated," I replied.

"Terminated?" Blake seemed worried.

"I think if we keep an eye on our dates and the progress of the development teams, we should have no problem controlling our primary constraint, which is time," I reassured him.

We continued through the project schedule before breaking for lunch. I was glad to have that portion complete as it seemed to be the most exhausting.

After lunch, I was happy to pass the torch to Jessica, who reviewed the change control process. She noted the good news that Matt designed a program to automate the change control process, making it easier to submit and monitor changes.

I made sure to make note of the scope freeze date, which I had to explain to Blake several times.

"So there are no changes after month four?" Blake asked a third time.

"No changes." I tried to stick to my guns. "That's a very critical point for our project and changes could really keep us from making the deadline."

Blake tried to throw around some scenarios to create one where I would say changes were okay. I tried to think of a way to help Blake understand the purpose of the scope freeze.

"How important is it for you to make your announcement at the banquet?" I asked.

"Oh, I must make my announcement," Blake answered with conviction.

"Well, the more changes we accept after month four, the less likely you will be able to make that important announcement," I said, leaning against the conference table.

"You have my support," Blake said, sounding like a team player and flashing his tennis instructor smile.

The second half of the meeting was a breeze. When I further explained how changes could cause the project to incur additional costs, I knew I had his full support.

The discussion was a nice transition into my next document review.

I explained how my budget was broken into two parts: one for resources and the second for outsourcing and miscellaneous.

Resources	Month 1			Month 2			Month 3		
	Hours	nº person	Total Hrs	Hours	nº person	Total Hrs	Hours	nº person	Total Hrs
Project Manager	90	1	90	80	1	80	80	1	80
Project Coordinator	45	1	45	45	1	45	45	1	45
Business Analyst	80	1	80	10	1	10	10	1	10
Senior Business Director	40	1	40	20	1	20			
Marketing Coordinator	20	1	20	20	1	20	20	1	20
IT Coordinator	45	1	45	120	1	120	120	1	120
Progammers									
Selection Committee				5	5	25	10	5	50
Resource Totals	$16,000			$16,000			$16,250		

I didn't show all the detail because I knew the

vendors were all ears. I did note that we were a little under budget but were continuing to look for ways to save with our final number being at $270,500.

"Does that include contingency?" Blake asked, concerned.

"No, but it does include my risk funding, so approximately $5,000 may go untouched."

This made Blake happy to know that he could stay under budget. I thought it might also be beneficial to share a chart that highlighted where the money was being spent.

This way Blake and Michael could see the bulk of the funding was zoned for Phase II, which covered the actual development of the demos. This meant that most of the costs were operational and zoned for our internal teams.

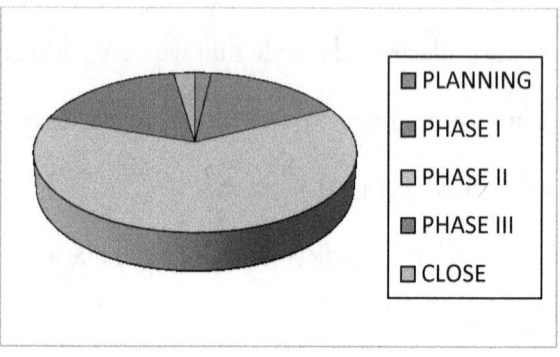

The second largest portion of the budget was for the Showcasing Banquet and Blake did not seem too displeased with that.

"How are we coming with the entertainment?" Blake asked.

I glanced over at Rej, who had not given me an update.

"Still conducting some research to see what our budget can afford," Rej said, looking through his notes.

Blake nodded his head, with an expression that clearly showed he had hoped for more information.

I could feel myself smile on the inside as I neared

the end of my meeting. I managed to keep everyone awake and everyone seemed excited to get started with the work.

After the meeting, Jessica and I reviewed all captured action items and uploaded them to our system, where they could be monitored.

I was proud of the results of my planning, but I knew from past experience that solid planning wasn't the only thing needed to run a successful project.

8   THE NEGOTIATION

The sun was beaming down on me as I sat at the light, waiting to pull into the Game Over parking lot. I thought about the lunch I had planned with Cindy later that afternoon.

"Oh my goodness!" I screamed happily as if the world was listening.

One of our advertisements was on the side of a stopped bus and I was overwhelmed with the excitement of seeing the ad in the real world...not just on a printout at the office.

I caught the end of the bus with my camera phone and sent a quick picture to Rej.

The team had been thrust into Phase 1 of the project with a very small transition period. Rej had done an excellent job on the marketing materials and we were able to use the company account to expand our reach for the target market.

The applications were pouring in faster than the selection committee could review them and I was trying to re-develop the process so they didn't become overwhelmed.

The senior business director, Michael, had to fight just about everyone when he put the committee together because everyone felt worthy enough to be a part of the big competition. The bottom line was who had the time.

Once in the office, I prepared for a status call where I wanted to determine, most importantly, the demographics needed for the Consumer Group. Michael still had not prepared the information. To my growing frustrations, he had become less participatory than he was at the beginning and harder to locate with each passing day.

I reached into my handbag in search of my ringing cell phone. I could tell it was the company cell, because it had a different ringtone.

At first, I was excited and felt slightly important

when I was handed a smartphone, until I found out it was a gift attached to my third project.

I would be responsible for my first technology project that involved the movement of company servers. I was told it would be a small and simple project, but when Willy chuckled during the meeting, I knew there would be surprises.

"Hello."

"Joyce Davis?" the voice on the other end wanted to confirm.

"Yes, this is she."

"Hi, Joyce. This is Mary Ann from the convention center. I'm calling to see if you were able to confirm the date for your banquet. I can't hold the rooms much longer."

I was so frustrated just at the thought of not being able to answer the question. I had been trying to work with Michael to determine the setup needs for break out rooms during the voting for the games.

"Hello? Ya there?" Mary Ann had somewhat of a southern drawl. I thought I remembered her speaking of growing up in the south.

I wanted to make an executive decision, but I didn't have the venue selection process slated until later in the project. Now Mary Ann was rushing my schedule.

"We will take it," I said with a sigh and a knot in my stomach the size of my new smartphone. I figured if I had too many rooms I could just cancel and forfeit a partial deposit; better to have them and not need them than the other way around.

I ended the call with Mary Ann to dial into my scheduled conference call with my team. I waited for beeps that would indicate others had joined the call. The sound of silence gave me a much-needed opportunity to check my email.

"Jessica," a recorded voice rang after a beep. That

girl was always on time.

More silence. Five minutes in and still no one else joined. I leaned my head outside my office to see if I could spot members of my team. I was less worried about them and more concerned about Michael joining, as he was the one with the information I so desperately needed.

After fifteen minutes of silence, I let Jessica drop the call and sent two emails. One email was to remind my team the importance of joining meetings... on time. The second was to remind Michael, again, that I needed critical information from him in order to keep the project moving forward.

I decided to walk down to the IT group early. I had a meeting with the group manager to determine the availability of the programmers that would be paired with the selection of candidates.

I couldn't believe we were already in our second month of phase 1.

I stopped at one of the big green leather couches to glance at my email on my phone which vibrated all day long, reminding me of nonstop communication. This time, it was Michael.

> Hey!
> I have fifteen minutes if you want to stop by now to chat.

Glancing at the time on my phone I hopped on the closest elevator and rode it to the top floor. If I could meet with Michael before my programmer meeting, I would be better prepared.

I sat down in Michael's office, feeling disheveled and unprepared. I didn't feel like I was capable of using complete sentences during the brief, unscheduled meeting with Michael. My mind was racing and at any moment, I knew he would glance at his expensive watch or wall clock signaling the end of my time.

"Banquet?" I panted, not taking the time to catch

my breath.

"Yes." Michael chuckled at my inability to calm down. "You can move forward with the rooms on hold."

Yes! I had made the right decision.

"For the programmers—outsource or internal?"

"Where are we on the budget?" Michael asked.

"Very close to being right on budget but it doesn't include my contingency," I offered.

"Not smart to use your contingency on outsourcing programmers. They are a high-ticket item. We only use a $50 per hour rate for our programmers, correct?"

"Yes," I responded, although Michael was clear on the answer.

"Outsourcing might triple that figure. Let's work with the programming manager to see who is available internally," Michael stated while pulling some information up on his computer.

Now I was the one looking at my watch.

"Consumer Group," I blurted with a blank face.

"Working on it. I know we're late but we will have it to you by the end of the week." Michael confirmed.

I wondered if my team might have questions. I scanned my mind for any other needs that had risen from past meetings but came up blank.

I thanked Michael for his time and dashed for an open elevator. They always seemed to take forever when I was in a rush and I needed to make it to the other side of the building in less than five minutes.

I had never been to the programmers' area. It mimicked a cocoon of busy worker bees flying to and fro with no visual indication, to an outsider, of exactly what was going on.

Their space was even more colorful than the rest of the building. The very large computer monitors were lit up with both bright and dark colors and all of the cubicle walls were covered with Game Over paraphernalia.

I asked several zombie look-alikes with their faces fixated on the screen where I could find the manager. Through muffled, mouth-filled and transfixed looks I gathered over there and eventually over there got me to a tiny office almost smaller than mine.

"Hello." I leaned inside the open door.

"Hi." A hand outstretched to meet mine.

"Pete?"

I glanced around the bustling room and wondered how in the world I would be able to ask this man for five of his busy team members.

"You're Joyce, right?" I nodded. "So I glanced at your email with your charter and such. What exactly do you need from me?" He got right to the point.

"I need five of your top programmers to pair with our candidates during Phase II of my project, which is the demo development."

"My top guys to babysit? No way! Can't do it."

I was speechless. I wasn't sure how to respond, much less negotiate for what I needed.

He continued, "Everyone on my team is over-allocated. All of my guys are running about three projects each and are fully booked. There's no way I can loan them out."

"But I don't even need them full time," I pleaded.

"Doesn't matter."

This guy was really good at standing his ground and he wasn't budging.

"You can outsource some programmers at about $150 per hour."

"My budget can't afford that and they won't know our system and how we work. Who will train them?"

I was becoming frustrated. Pete only shrugged his shoulders, not offering any viable suggestions.

A lanky guy with baggy jeans twice his size came in with a question. While Pete excused himself, I sent a quick text message to Charles, praying that he would quickly respond.

I fumbled around with my phone, pretending to check email while the two men yammered on about technical stuff I couldn't make out.

C'mon Charles, I thought as I peered up hoping the interruption would take longer that I would normally be pleased with.

"Excuse us," Pete said, leading the tall and lanky man out of the office and back into the throng of busy bees.

I quickly found Charles in my contacts and dialed.

I turned my body around in the small desk chair as not to be heard. There was so much noise out in the beehive I could have screamed and they still would have paid me no attention.

"Heading to a meeting," Charles answered.

"Sorry. I'm in a bind; the manager of the

programmers will not budge on giving me the five programmers I need and I can't afford to outsource." I said it all in a hurry.

As I tried not to be discovered, Charles gave me some quick tips on how I needed to negotiate and figure out what I had that Pete wanted.

"If all else fails, use the CEO. Gotta go."

Charles hung up the phone before I could ask what he meant. I felt bad when I bothered him during his work day; especially after his promotion.

"The CEO Blake?" I muttered in confusion as Pete sauntered back into the office.

"Is there anything else I can do for you?"

"Well, I was going to ask you the same thing. Is there some way I can convince you to find time to loan me your guys for 120 days?"

"I don't know what to tell you," was his only reply.

"Listen. They are only providing guidance. It's not

like they have to do actual work. I have reserved workstations for the candidates and they will have 120 days total to meet their deadlines. So it means the programmers you loan me won't have to sit for 8 hours a day with a candidate working on their demo."

Pete sat expressionless.

"I'll even arrange to have your programmer's workstations relocated so they can work on their daily responsibilities while they mentor."

I was hoping to get a nudge. When I realized that Pete was not the least bit interested in playing into my negotiations, I blurted, "I guess I'll just ask Blake if he can give me more money because you are unable to make it work."

I got up to leave.

"Hold on." Pete turned to the computer holding his hand up to stop me.

I waited in agony, hoping he had a credible

solution.

"Give me a couple of days and I'll see what I can pull together."

"Perfect," I said trying not to smile as big as I felt.

9 THE STATUS

The fasten seatbelt sign lit up as I wiggled around, trying to get comfortable in my coach airline seat.

I bet Blake doesn't fly coach, I thought as I pulled my laptop out to see what I could work on during my flight.

With everything going on with the competition, I needed to fly out to Chicago for my server project. Apparently it was important for me to be onsite for the move.

At least, the server project was moving along quickly. I needed at least one project to end before I was assigned anything else.

"I need you to close that for take-off," the flight attendant said, politely referring to my newly-opened laptop.

I complied and took out my study guide to review some material. On top of it all, I was trying my hardest to study for the PMP and pass the exam before the content was updated yet another time.

The flight seemed long as I read through the boring textbook, trying to find the best way to remember formulas.

I had one carry-on bag, which made it easier to pick up my rental car after landing and head straight to my hotel to brace myself for what I felt would be a long three days.

After a rough night's sleep, an early morning brought me a continental breakfast, a suit that fit snugly from the increase of pounds, and a data center tour by a guy who appeared as if he had not seen the sun in a long time.

I sat at a small table, waiting for the assigned project resources to arrive. Signing into Game Over's VPN, I quickly went through my email to see if anything needed my attention.

Michael sent an email on the consumer group, which meant Rej could move forward with the selection process and I could mark policies and procedures complete for Phase I.

As I sifted through 58 unread emails, I found I could mark a few tasks complete. The selection committee approved my new applicant review process and Max provided an update on the development for automating the voting process.

Finally, I came upon the long-awaited email from Pete with the list of programmers for the competition. I read Pete's very short email with excitement, glad I did not have to ask Blake for additional funding.

> Hi Joyce,
> Per your request, here is a list of programmers
> assigned to your project:
> Sam Lincoln
> Lucy Jim

Brian Yolk

Jason Peters

Bruce Holstein.

No way! No way. No way, I thought. How did Bruce's name end up on the programmer's list? He was a BA.

I quickly sent an email to Pete, praying with every word that he had made a terrible mistake. There was no way I could work with Bruce again. I avoided him with every move I made in the office.

I waited impatiently for a response from Pete and the end of the day came without happy news. I documented the progress of my local server team and returned to the hotel to an empty, quiet space that was much lonelier than my apartment back home.

I thought of ways I could get rid of Bruce without anyone knowing. Who would really miss him after all?

The next day came with a few hiccups and I found

myself more involved in the process of moving the servers. The server project wasn't that exciting but I was learning a lot about the technical side of things.

During one of the breaks, I tried to quickly check my email. I accidentally expressed some frustration aloud.

"You okay, Boss?" one of the tech guys asked.

"Just waiting on someone to respond to my email," I smiled, trying to redirect my attention.

"Have you tried calling? No one ever picks up the phone anymore."

I thought of how stupid I felt always waiting for an email and never actually having tried calling. I pulled out my work cell phone and gave Pete a call.

"Pete talking."

"Hi, Pete. It's Joyce. I was calling because I wanted to follow up on my email I sent regarding the list of programmers you offered. I think a mistake was made because Bruce Holstein is listed."

"No mistake. He's cross-training in my department and I thought this would be the perfect opportunity for him."

"Ummm." I had no words.

"Listen. It was hard to come up with five people. You are lucky to have Bruce on the team."

I beg to differ, I thought. After my call with Pete, I decided to use the remainder of my time on site in Chicago to research vendors for the sound and lighting requirements for the showcase banquet.

I also sent an email invitation to all of the programmers so Jessica and I could brief them on the process and expectations for the competition.

I left Chicago feeling much worse than I did when I landed. I spent my entire flight with my head buried in my study book, thinking that passing the PMP might help me escape Bruce if necessary.

***

The office was just as I had left it with all its craziness and buzz. Rosie was still planted atop of her exercise ball and Amber was still the office grouch.

"We need to talk." Max walked into my office before I could get settled.

I didn't respond; I only leaned my head to the side with my hand rested on my hip, wondering what he could possibly have to tell me so early in the morning.

"There's a glitch in the voting system and we have a shortage on the loaner equipment for the candidates."

"Which system and how short?" I prepared for the worst.

"The committee's voting system and we need two more towers and four additional large monitors."

"Has the room already been prepped?" I asked, turning on my computer so I could open the risk management document.

"Not sure. My eyes are on equipment only," Matt

said, waiting for a response that would actually help him.

I felt like I was sinking and was making too many decisions with very little information.

"Schedule an emergency meeting with the vendor and see if you can get a manager on the call," I said with a sigh. "I'll work on the monitors and towers."

I took out my project planner and jotted down the action item and decided to grab a coffee from the lounge while my laptop came to life.

"Hey there." I heard a distinct voice.

"Hi." For once I was glad to see Blake.

"How's our project?" he asked while ordering some form of a veggie smoothie.

"We are moving right along," I said. "I'm glad I saw you here. We're short on towers and monitors for the candidates in the loaner department. I think it's best to use some of our contingency budget."

I had gotten savvy in my conversations with Blake,

learning to make statements instead of asking questions.

"Do what you must. Just as long as it finishes on time."

"Sure thing! No problem." I removed the lid on my coffee.

"I was thinking," Blake stood about to offer one of his grand thoughts, "we should have gifts for all of the voters?"

"Gifts, sir?"

"Nothing big," Blake said, smiling innocently, "just something to say thank you."

"That will be a huge impact to our budget," I pleaded.

"Use the contingency. Besides, we must give gifts. Ooh, let's do door prizes too."

Blake certainly had the wrong idea about the contingency budget.

"But—" I started.

"It's not month four!" He waved his index finger as he walked away from me before stopping to ask. "Do you have some sort of status report?"

"Yes. I post them every week and I send you an email with the link." I peered over the rim of my coffee cup.

Was he serious? As much time as I spent working on those status reports, he wasn't even reading them?

"Go ahead and send me another copy. I'm sure everything's fine. I hear the project is practically running itself." Blake grinned, showing his newly-whitened teeth.

I almost choked on my sip of very warm coffee as I watched Blake saunter off exuding the confidence he flared so well.

I rushed to my desk to download a copy of the most recent status report. It was a quick one-page document. Michael had recommended that I create a one-page status report for Blake, keeping it simple and easy to follow.

Dr. A. Arrington

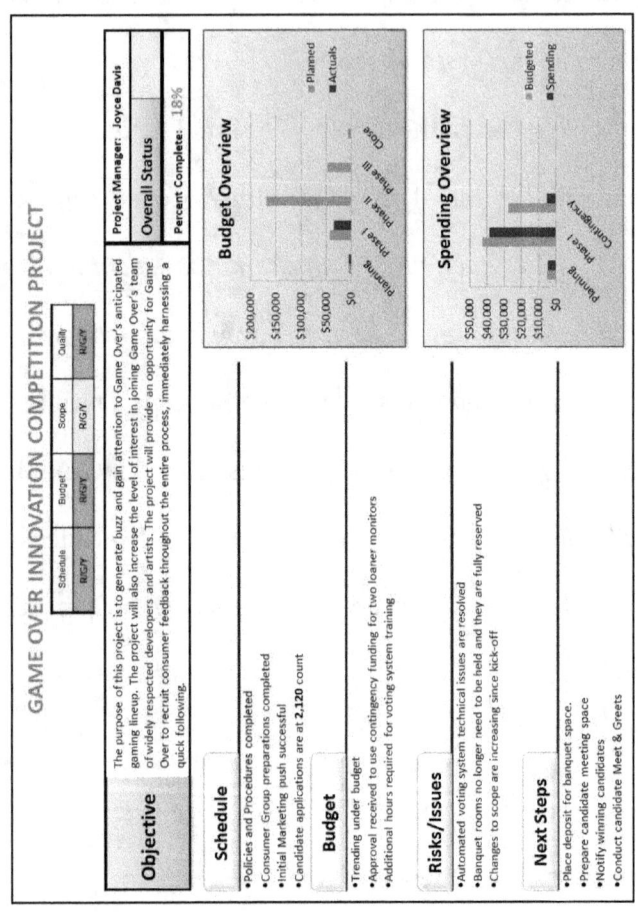

I made a few last-minute updates based on

changes and progress that had occurred since the last

status report was posted. I decided to also send Blake a link to the change form for his most recent 'great' idea.

Just as I was clicking the send button, Max barged into my office.

"I've been looking for you! Can you meet in five minutes?" Matt asked.

He had been able to locate one of the vendor managers regarding the system glitches. The only problem was he wanted to meet immediately. Sooner than I expected.

"Five minutes?"

"The only manager available for the next week and a half is available in five minutes."

I ran to my desk and checked my calendar. I usually blocked off time in the morning to catch up on email or prepare my status reports for the end of the week.

I made time for the impromptu meeting and asked Matt to quickly brief me on the problem. During the call, the vendor was confident they could fix the issue.

"We have to research the problem and we should have an answer by the end of the day," the manager bellowed into the phone.

"Please contact Matt as soon as you have an update. We need to know how long the fix will take. We are supposed to announce our winners soon."

"I understand, Miss. My people are on it and we will have an update to you by close of business."

The call ended. In retrospect, I should have asked which close of business day he would have an answer, because an entire week went by without a word from the vendor.

I was on the verge of having Max replace the vendor, when they finally called with good news.

I immediately notified the selection committee who had been patiently waiting to start casting their electronic ballots. In less than a week, they would be expected to vote on thousands of submissions, ultimately coming to a decision on the top five candidates.

10   THE ANNOUNCEMENT

"Welcome! You represent the top five candidates from thousands of ideas submitted for our first ever Gaming Innovation Competition." Blake started his speech as his voice filled every corner of the auditorium.

I thought it would be best if he kicked off the small event where we announced the five selected candidates for the competition. I was not one for speaking in front of large crowds and it seemed as if the entire company was gathered in the auditorium to get a glimpse at the competition's finalists.

Blake had a well-prepared and somewhat lengthy presentation. The announcement of the finalists had not been as grandiose as he had wanted; but I reminded Blake that the budget had increased due to his recent changes and it was best to keep it simple.

Once Blake had completed his presentation, Michael spoke for a few minutes about technicalities before turning it over to me.

By the time I reached the microphone, most of the crowd had died down, leaving mostly my team, the candidates and the Programmers.

As I began to discuss the importance of the relationship between the programmers and the candidates, I heard someone shouting over me.

"Will the sessions be catered?"

When I realized it was my arch-nemesis, Bruce, I elected to ignore him, which seemed to work well in the past.

"If you remember nothing else, remember your deadline. It is very important to work with your assigned programmer to meet the timeline of the demo development or you could be eliminated from the competition," I began.

I took a deep breath and continued. "The first step that you will need to complete is selecting an artist candidate for your team. Once your team is complete, you will need to work with your assigned programmer to create your schedules."

"When does the fun start?" Bruce asked, raising his hand this time.

"The assignment of programmers will be random and will be done shortly."

I made the executive decision to randomly assign programmers, because I could not in good conscience assign Bruce to a team, as that would be an automatic death wish.

Once I concluded my short speech, Max was to show the candidates how to review the artist portfolios online to make a final selection. While he scattered, I saw Jessica working the crowd to answer questions.

I interrupted Rej posting images of his new baby on his social media page to ask him about the updates on the gifts. Surprisingly, Blake had already submitted and approved his own change request for voter gifts and we needed to implement the change right away.

"Do you have any cost estimates on the favors?"

"Umm," Rej startled, "I'm waiting to hear back from a couple of vendors."

I wanted to have the information to update my presentation for my gateway review. We were at the end of Phase 1 and while I knew Blake wouldn't pull the plug on his precious project, I wanted my information to be spotless.

The gateway presentation template was very similar to a kick-off in that it was long and filled with details about the project. Lucky for me I had kept up with my status reports and all I had to do was transfer the information.

While I was chatting away with Rej and, waiting for the five candidates to go through the system review with Max, Tracy rushed into the auditorium with a concerned look.

"I need to talk to you," Tracy bellowed, coming near me.

We quickly walked to a space that was not occupied by others. He spoke quietly and I could barely follow what he was saying.

"Did you confirm the generator health for the servers that were moved?"

My head was spinning. I was trying to get on the same page as Tracy but found it quite difficult to readjust my thought pattern.

"Yes or no?" he demanded.

I was very surprised at his tone and searched my head quickly.

"Yes! I remember having the discussion with one of the on-site guys," I said, happy to provide an answer.

"We are having some major issues with the new location," he said, hands on hips and looking around in open space for answers.

I had nothing to do with where the servers were placed; I only managed the move. I thought I was free and clear of the project.

"I need the names of your on-site team members."

I quickly searched my email and provided Tracy with the information he required.

Tracy left the room as quickly as he had appeared and I was glad to be moving on. I made a mental note to never get on his bad side.

I sat back looking at my team. They seemed to be coming together well. They were all mingling among each other and helping the candidates, not needing much direction from me.

I stole a quick glance at Bruce, who seemed to be on good behavior for now.

***

By the end of the week, all of the candidates had

selected artists and I was able to pass my gateway review with a breeze. I was still under budget but was not surprised when Blake asked me why overall status was yellow.

I told him that his changes to the scope caused the project to go yellow, but now that we had reached the scope freeze deadline, we should be okay.

He didn't seem too happy, but I wasn't sure if it was that he could no longer make changes or that he was the reasoning behind the yellow status.

Tracy stopped me after my successful gateway meeting and congratulated me on a job well done. He also congratulated me on a newly assigned project to manage installation of gaming kiosks. He said he thought I was ready to take on more responsibility.

I was surprised. Then again, my process improvement project was moving at snail's pace and the competition project was in a coasting period.

After my gateway, I was prepared for the first meeting with my team since we started Phase II. My project was only at 22% but I felt like we should have been somewhere close to 80%. It seemed like it took one month for my project to move 1%. It was exhausting.

Moving forward, the chosen programmers would be joining our team in meetings and it was always my goal to keep it at 30 minutes. This meant cutting out the chit chat. I pulled together a simple standing agenda.

- What's New?
- Review the Project Schedule
- Review Project Risks
- Update Action Items
- Discuss Next Steps
- Questions

All other PMs on my team held 15-minute standing meetings and I was not clear on how that was even possible.

"Welcome everyone! Let's get started," I began as Rej was the last to enter.

Most of the programmers joined on the phone, except for one who came into the conference room I managed to reserve.

"We are a couple of weeks into Phase II of our project, programmers and artists are paired with developers and we have officially selected catering and entertainment for the showcase banquet."

There were mild cheers across the room. There were also a few coming from me.

"Does anyone else have anything new to add?"

"I have good news," Jessica chimed in.

"Tell us!" I said, hoping to keep the meeting moving along.

"Well, I wanted to save it for our personal team meeting, but I can't keep it in. Yesterday I passed my PMP exam." Jessica squealed.

Disappointment filled my face, but I tried desperately not to show it. I had hardly studied for the exam and here Jessica, my assistant, had studied, taken and passed it.

"Congratulations," I stammered as those around the room gave Jessica words of encouragement.

"Now you can take Joyce's job," I heard Bruce say over the conference line.

I cleared my throat, offered up one last congratulatory comment before moving on and trying not to sound too bitter. Instead of being upset, I decided to use it as inspiration to get back on track.

"It looks like you are all done with requirement specifications, Nancy. Good job," I said, trying to sound as cheerful as possible as I shared the project schedule on the projection screen.

"It was a challenge, but I think everything went well," Nancy smiled.

I had been concerned that Bruce would give Nancy a hard time since she was, in fact, his replacement. I assumed everything was going well since she had not mentioned anything.

After Nancy's update, I mostly spoke with the programmers, asking them about their status and progress with candidate teams.

"Everything is going great," one programmer chimed in.

"We are having a hard time finding time to meet, but we are still on schedule," another added.

"My team is kicking ass," Bruce came in loud and clear. "Just finished our wireframes last night."

That would mean Bruce's team was ahead of schedule. Should I rejoice or keep moving? Apparently he was a better programmer than BA. Go figure.

I noted the progress within the project schedule and tried to keep my mind focused on the meeting and off of Jessica.

I quickly reviewed our risks for the current phase, asking everyone to keep an eye out for triggers. Next, I covered the team's action items.

"Rej, any news on the prizes?"

"Which prizes?" Rej asked, looking up from his laptop.

I was sure he was not listening, but instead was on some social media site. I would complain, but he always turned his work in on time.

"All prizes," I stated, trying to show my seriousness in getting the meeting over with.

"Oh yeah. Well, I located a large check vendor and I was able to get you concrete price points, finally, for the voter gifts," Rej delivered over the top of his laptop.

"Please send those as soon as the meeting is over," I asked, curtly feeling my temperature rise.

I brushed through the remainder of the meeting quicker than usual and tidied up the meeting room for the next occupant. As I was leaving, I was met at the door by Tracy. Jessica was trying very hard to hide in his shadow.

This can't be good, I thought. Had she noticed my disdain for her newly announced accomplishment?

"You got a minute?" Tracy asked. Not waiting for an answer, he barged into the conference room followed by my old shadow.

We all sat around the large conference table, me on one side alone and Tracy and Jessica on the other.

"I'm sure by now you've heard Jessica's good news," Tracy stated, cupping his hands over the table as Jessica grinned from ear to ear.

"Yes."

"Well, I've decided to place her in a junior PM role

to help ramp up our team for the many projects that will be headed our way."

My mouth hit the table on its way to the floor.

"So she will be working on the gaming projects?" I asked, slightly disconnected from the real world.

"Yes, and I want to get her started as soon as possible so she will begin to transition next week."

"Ok," was the only word I remembered how to pronounce.

"You've been a great mentor," Jessica started before being cut off by Tracy.

"I think it's best for you to start to take over her duties until further notice," Tracy said.

"So I won't be getting a replacement?"

"I don't have it in my budget to hire anyone new right now; so at the moment, no." Tracy concluded the brief meeting.

I felt far removed from the table. I only began to

return mentally after Leslie entered the room looking for dry erase markers.

"You good?" Leslie asked.

She had proven to be one of the less dramatic PMs of the bunch, mostly keeping to herself and staying out of everyone's business.

"I think I just had my assistant taken away," I said blankly.

"Oh, yeah. I heard about that."

"How? It just happened." I was stunned and even more lost than before.

"That's right, you don't know," Leslie said, smiling.

As she searched the conference room for blue, green and red erasable markers, Leslie quietly told me about the rumors regarding Tracy and Amber.

Tracy had promised Amber my innovative gaming project and a promotion but never delivered on either promise. Apparently whatever affair they had, ended when

I was hired. Shortly after Tracy started another office affair with Jessica.

"Did Amber start as an assistant too?" I asked, being drawn into the office gossip.

"Oh no. She came from one of the top IT firms about a year before Tracy. Most of us have been here longer than he has."

"But I thought the PMO was new?" I asked, even more confused.

"The PMO is new, but us PMs are not," Leslie said, laughing, before leaving me in the conference room to ponder over all the information she had dumped on me.

I hated gossip and didn't want to believe I had lost my assistant to some tawdry office affair.

I crawled back to my office, closed the door and buried my head in my PMP study guide.

11 THE SYSTEM

I was sitting outside the office near the entrance gate to Game Over, waiting for my sister and Thad to show up. I was treating them to a tour and free lunch on me in our main cafeteria.

Besides, if it wasn't for them, I wouldn't have the job. I wasn't being cheap, but with all the new money I was making, Uncle Sam was taking most and the rest was going to catching up on bills and saving for a new car.

I loved my car, Frank, but I wasn't sure how much longer he could hang on.

"Hey, sis!" Stacy squealed. Thad looked partially impressed as he strode in, hands in his pockets.

I signed them in at the front desk and after they were garnished with visitor badges, our first stop was the gaming hall that showcased the history of games created at Game Over.

I walked past the auditorium but I explained to

Thad and Stacy that they would not be allowed in because of all the top secret work I was doing.

"The competition that is posted on billboards all over the city is now top secret?" Thad joked.

"Well, the competition may not be top secret, but what's going behind those doors sure is," I smiled.

The truth was that it was pretty amazing what happened behind those doors. Since the second phase of the project began, my team and I moved into the space to be available to the candidates.

In the process of sitting with each other, month after month in one room, we got to know one another pretty well and became quite close.

We even started to develop relationships with the programmers and the candidates as they came and went.

"This food is amazing," Stacy said, taking another bite from her chicken salad sandwich."

"I know! They don't skimp on the rationing either,"

Thad added.

"I'm glad you like it. I really appreciate you forcing me to meet with Charles. If it hadn't been for you guys, I'd probably still be broke and depressed."

"Well, if you really want to repay us..." Stacy started.

"What?"

Stacy stared at Thad and then back at me.

"What?!" I was becoming impatient.

Stacy held out her hand to reveal a nicely-sized diamond ring.

"You can plan our wedding!" she almost screamed.

We both squealed and jumped up and down in the middle of the lunch area. I knew onlookers were probably startled by our display of excitement, but I couldn't hold it in.

"Congratulations," I said over and over again to the both of them. "But I'm not a wedding planner."

"How hard can it be?" Stacy said happily. "If you can plan a whole competition, I'm sure you can handle a small destination wedding in the Caribbean." They both smiled.

After lunch, I was back in the auditorium updating my project documents and responding to emails. Two of the candidates were working away at their demos.

Rej and Max were off to the side having a meeting about the creative and technical aspects of the demo presentations.

"The A-team is in the building," I heard Bruce announce as the large auditorium doors opened.

The teams were all sitting at individual tables and the large monitors seemed to take over the room. We tried to create as much privacy as possible, but when everyone was present, the noise increased and productivity decreased.

"How many hours do I have left, Boss?" one of the

programmers asked me.

Boss had become my nickname and not one I was fond of. I went from fetching coffee to someone calling me boss and it was a bit embarrassing.

"One sec."

When we first began, I broke the project down into hours and each programmer was given approximately 40 hours per month. They all told me immediately it wasn't nearly enough time to contribute, but I assured them that they were only overseers.

The forty hours went quickly as each programmer was drawn to the auditorium wanting to put in more than what they originally anticipated.

I pulled up my project schedule and budget to run some quick numbers to determine how many hours he had left.

"Fifteen for this month," I said with a wince.

"Fifteen? Is that all?"

They were all disappointed when they reached the end of their time, but later found that they could continue to work; it would just have to be off record and off the clock.

"Get your ass down here," I heard a loud voice. The entire room halted to the booming voice and we realized that it was coming from one of the programmers who had their phone on speaker.

"Gotta go," the programmer said, sprinting from the room.

"Looks like somebody's in trouble," Bruce said.

Bruce was still a problem but not in the way I had expected. His team was moving along at a great pace and it was because he didn't belong anywhere, so he had nowhere to be but in the auditorium.

He was able to spend the entire day in the auditorium, bugging me and helping his team and even working when his team was absent.

After some digging, I found out that when Bruce was removed from my team, he was left without a project. Like me, no one wanted to work with him, not even his precious friend Willy. The others only pretended he was great long enough to pawn him off on someone else.

Why is he still here? I wondered and after digging a little deeper I found that he had several relatives, high up in the organization... the board maybe, and he was the bad apple on the family tree.

After I found out all the juicy details it made it much easier to ignore him and not worry about getting rid of him.

The lights flickered and just as I glanced at Matt, I heard an, "Oh no!"

One of the candidates was yelling. Apparently the flickering had temporarily knocked out the towers and someone had lost their work.

"My presentation is gone!" he screamed.

We all sat in silence, not really knowing what to say or how to help.

"Give me a sec," Matt said, leaving the room.

While Matt was gone, I tried to calm the guy down with reassuring words and a soothing tone, but he soon left to get some fresh air. He had been working all day on his presentation and it had disappeared from the desktop.

Matt re-entered the room shortly after the candidate returned from his quick breather. Matt was trailed by a guy holding some gadgets.

"Usually, our systems are prepared to immediately backup when things like this happen," Matt said as they hooked some doohickeys up to the computer tower.

"That's good news," I said, leaning over and smiling with my hands on my knees as if I were talking to a group of kindergartners with boo-boos.

"If this works, we should be able to recover everything that was on this tower."

The candidate just stood there, with his hands shoved deep into the abyss of his pockets, waiting for any news to subside his anxiety.

Matt and the newcomer must have worked on the system for hours before finally restoring the work and allowing the poor candidate to sit back down and continue where he left off.

He was very grateful that he even shed a few tears before feverishly wiping them away, so as not to appear soft in front of the other guys.

Matt patted him on the back and said, "Man, I understand," before he and his silent helper left the room just as quickly as they had entered.

The presentations were just as important as the demo, because it allowed the candidates an opportunity to engage the voters in the entire game, especially areas that would not be experienced during the demo.

"Crazy day!" Rej said, as if he had bad news.

"What's wrong?" I asked, expecting the worst.

"The entertainment Blake selected is not returning my phone calls and I'm trying to confirm them before approving the invitation."

"I'll reach out to Blake's assistant to see if she can help us out."

I sent Maggie a quick ping on the instant message system and when she didn't respond, I sent an email, hoping she could pull some strings to help us out.

We were getting closer and closer to the banquet and things were becoming more and more complicated. I felt like all of the days were running together and I didn't know my own name half of the time.

When the clock struck five, I pulled out my PMP study guide and began to review formulas and memorize inputs and outputs. The information was a lot easier to consume now that I was an actual project manager.

I sat in the auditorium until 8 p.m. and watched

candidates come and go, working hard, determined to out code their competitors. It was nice to see how committed they were to meeting my strict deadlines.

I locked my computer up in my office before saying goodnight to RP, the night guard. I walked through the nearly deserted parking lot towards Frank, noting the few cars that indicated work was still being done inside.

12   THE ISSUES

I was meeting with Nancy, trying to get a grip on our new project and working to see if I could continue to offload some of Jessica's work between the two of us. I realized I was not on Tracy's high priority list for receiving a replacement for Jessica.

Nancy had come from one of the competing gaming companies and she was used to the upbeat culture of our office. She was such a team player, always willing to step up and take on extra work.

She had worked extremely hard with the candidates to help develop their requirement specifications and now she was willing to help me. She had confided in me that she too was interested in becoming a project manager and hoped that she could learn from me.

Our new kiosk project was much more complicated than I expected, with lots more vendor involvement than the competition project. The idea had been submitted by a new leader with big dreams and a tiny budget.

The concept was to create a virtual experience of our games through these specially-designed kiosks. Instead of sending in our demo games like all the other companies, there would be a kiosk that featured our complete new line-up.

"I think we should first see what the vendor pricing is before we make any other decisions," I said to Nancy as she took notes. "Do you know how many total kiosks we are installing?"

"There isn't a solid number, but somewhere around 150," Nancy replied.

I could only imagine the number of problems that could arise from me having to visit 150 stores to make sure they could host one of our kiosks.

"Hello, ladies." Rej interrupted our meeting to share the initial concepts for the banquet invitations.

"These look amazing." Nancy was always very

supportive and always smiling.

I had not taken any personal time, since I lost Jessica to Tracy and I felt like my virtual inbox pile wasn't getting any lighter.

"Looks like you heard from the entertainment," I said, teasing Rej as I reviewed his invitations.

"Finally." He looked so relieved.

"I think these are good enough to review with Blake. Why don't you set up a meeting for the three of us and we'll see if he can make a decision?"

My phone started to buzz and beep and I used Rej as an excuse to take a break.

I had received an email from one of the candidates about his relationship with his programmer.

Hello Joyce,

I am sorry to bother you but I wanted to bring it to your attention that my programmer has missed my last two meetings and I'm afraid I won't meet the deadline in three weeks.

"Shoot!" I said aloud.

"What's wrong?" Nancy asked, genuinely concerned.

I shook my head, not completely ready to discuss it with anyone.

I quickly repositioned my laptop and pulled up my list to double check which programmer was assigned to assist the candidate who sent the email.

In our last meeting, the same programmer stated that everything was on track but it looked like he was not completely honest. I knew the coding and programming would be the most difficult part of the project, but I never expected dishonesty.

I had just shared an all green status report, which meant my scope, budget and schedule were all progressing as planned. Although I was spending more on the programmers than I originally expected, I was still within my budget.

My project was past the 50% mark and had approximately $120,000 left to spend, including contingency, which meant there was not a lot of room for more surprises.

I phoned the programmer in question and he filled my ears with tons of excuses.

"Do we need to call on one of the alternates?" I asked, concerned.

"No. I can do it. I just had a couple of bad weeks," he pleaded.

Blake had apparently promised the programmers a secret bonus and rights to the chosen game in exchange for their participation. Lucky for me, it didn't have to come out of my budget, but it was something nice to hang over their heads.

"I promise, I'll work extra hard to make it up," he said.

I reminded him of the hours we had left in the budget and he promised not to go over. Just as I ended the call, Nancy returned with coffee for the both of us.

"Thanks! That was sweet of you," I said, cupping the warm cup between my hands.

"Where were we?" I asked, shuffling papers around trying to transition my thinking.

"Vendors!" Nancy smiled.

"Right. Do you think you are comfortable enough to handle the vendors for the competition and I can handle the vendors for the kiosk project?" I asked, making a face because I felt like I was asking for a lot.

"No, I'm o——"

"I need to speak to you." Bruce barged into my office.

"I'm in a meeting," I retorted, showing a sign of obviousness on my face.

"I really need to speak to you." Bruce sounded

serious and a little panicked.

"Let's take another five-minute break," I said to Nancy and she and Rej both left.

Without explaining, Bruce rushed me down to security because apparently a fight had broken out by two candidates.

Each blamed it on the other, saying one was trying to steal the other's idea. One thing consistent in both of their stories was the presence of good ol' Bruce.

I searched my mind, but could not recall any talks or training on how to handle the situation.

I wished I could call Charles, like when I first started at Game Over. My meetings with Charles had diminished to feverish texts and promises to meet for lunch. The small amount of free time I had, I spent trying to study for my certification.

Bruce broke into my thoughts when he grabbed me by the arm and pulled me to the side. I almost motioned for security myself.

"To be honest, it's my fault," he started, actually sounding sincere. "I got them all riled up with my jabbering and this is the result."

"Is that right?"

"Listen, Joyce. I know you have no reason to offer me any support, but I need this to work. I've been trying to get in this group for years and now's my chance. If it gets out that I started this ruckus, I'll never be allowed to be on the team."

I searched Bruce's eyes for some sign of humanity but all I could think of was how much grief he caused me day after day, month after month.

"Please," Bruce pleaded.

I think he was actually starting to cry. The two candidates sat slumped in the small security area, waiting for some direction.

"Please let me handle this," I asked the security

guards who were happy to relinquish imaginary control.

Bruce gave me a look that said, *thanks a thousand times.*

I walked quickly over to the equipment manager's office, whom I had made good friends with during one of my excursions out on the company lawn.

After a quick greeting, I asked him to set up temporary partitions in the open auditorium to separate the workspaces.

Bruce and I helped the equipment manager drag the unused partitions through Game Over's massive facility on two wobbly carts.

When we finally had everything set up, Bruce was singing a different tune.

"I don't know how to thank you Joyce," Bruce said. I could tell he was working to turn over a new leaf.

"I won't speak of this to anyone, under one condition," I said, holding up my index finger.

"Name it," Bruce conceded.

"You keep out of this room and let the other teams work in peace..."

"But how am I supposed to work with my team?" Bruce cut me off.

With my finger still raised and my eyes squinted, I made a statement that would make Bruce buckle at the knees, knowing I had won our battle and would be named master.

"A4!"

13   THE DEADLINE

"So why are we here?" Blake asked, looking more and more like a cartoon character as the days passed on.

"Because I need gateway approval," I said for the third time.

"It appears that a couple of the candidates have not completed their work," Tracy tried to explain. "We can either shut it down and move on with those who have finished, or move on and give those who haven't finished more time."

And it wasn't a couple of the candidates it was the same candidate that reached out to me stating his fears of not completing. If it had not been the end of the road, I would have had his very lazy and uncommitted programmer replaced.

At one point, I actually gave the candidate the option to switch programmers, but he declined.

After Tracy's explanation, Blake suddenly

understood everything.

"Ah, I get it," he said, swiveling in his chair until finally he stood with his hands on his hips.

Surprisingly all of the candidates had met their deadlines except for the one. Bruce's team actually finished ahead of time. All of the teams were pretty much wrapping up their banquet presentations.

"Let's do this," Blake had moved one hand from his hip to his chin. "Let's keep this ship moving and whoever's not ready by the banquet, can't present."

"But what about..." I started to ask about all of the printing material that was catered specifically to the candidate's demos before Tracy shushed me with his hand.

"Thanks, Blake, we will figure the rest out. So can we call this a go?" Tracy stood up to shake his hand.

"Why not?" Blake pumped out a laugh that sounded fake and like it belonged on the Lifetime Channel.

I was ready for a vacation and was planning time off after the project was over. I had not accumulated much vacation time, but I knew a couple of days away was all I needed to refresh.

Nancy, Matt, Rej and I were headed out to do a walk-thru of the facility and on my way out, I sent a rushed email to the candidate, giving him the good news that he could continue in the competition.

After later receiving emails from all of the candidates, I realized I accidentally sent the email to the entire group of candidates. I was bombarded with emails of the unfairness of the additional time given to the one candidate who had fallen behind.

My mistake was a sign that moving forward I needed to slow down and pay attention.

I also needed to phone a friend.

"Hey, stranger."

"Hi, Charles! It's been so long since I've spoken to

you," I said, smiling.

"How goes it, old friend?" he asked in his mentor-like tone.

"It goes," I said sharing familiar exchanges. "How's your new gig?"

"Amazingly challenging. I love it!"

"I'm so happy for you. Do you have time to help an old mentee?" I asked, hoping he had minutes to spare.

"Two minutes, but then I'm off to a business lunch date."

"Oooh fancy. I'll make it quick."

I explained to Charles my issue with my poor communication. I think I misused my two minutes by also adding in some complaints about missed sleep.

"In actuality, they all have the extra time; it just depends on how they use it. Frankly, the others are in a better position to put some final touches on their work," Charles said calmly, not rushing the conversation.

He always made some great points.

"Thanks. I think I can spin that a bit and make it work," I said. "I really appreciate your help during my first project."

"Anytime and thanks for the invite; I wouldn't miss your banquet for the moon," Charles said.

We ended the call and I thought about the best way to manage my last month before the big event. Phase II was at 93%, which meant my primary focus could be the banquet.

I walked into the conference hall amazed at the size of the space. We would have the main banquet room, with a connected break-out space for the voting stations.

I used the remaining $4,500 left from my original budget to hire additional staff to help Matt manage the voting stations during the banquet.

The event manager walked us through our event step by step, explaining sound, lighting and coordination.

She explained how we would have access to her team and provided additional information on how to access specific resources.

Since Blake insisted we use his favorite bistro for catering, we were also given a lecture on bringing in outside food.

In the middle of the event manager's presentation, I had to step away to take a call from Jessica.

"Hi, Joyce."

"Hi Jessica. I'm kind of in the middle of something."

"Oh, yeah, I'm sorry. I was hoping I could get you to take a look at my status report."

Although Jessica had moved on, it didn't stop her from asking me to help her out on her project duties. It seemed that Amber and Willy weren't too fond of her either.

"Sure, I'll take a look, but I gotta go," I said.

"I really miss my old team," Jessica said quietly before hanging up.

While I was upset how she left my team without any word or notice, I decided not to hold a grudge. I was so grateful for Charles that I wanted to offer someone else the same guidance if I could.

Besides Jessica was my eyes and ears to the inside information. How else would I find out so much great detail about Bruce?

After a very long walk-thru and a much-needed break, I decided to work from home for the remainder of the day. My team and I dispersed, saying our goodbyes, knowing there was so much to do in the little time left.

14 THE SHOWCASE

The day of the banquet had finally arrived. The last ten months had been the longest of my life. I woke with my hair matted to my face, having left the conference hall at 11 pm the previous night, finishing the final touches with my team.

We had revisited the conference hall several times after our initial visit and became very comfortable in the space.

It was necessary to complete an official a walk-thru of Rej's creatively crafted program to ensure we were prepared for the big night.

An Evening of Innovation

Welcome

Entertainment

Meal

Demo Presentations

Voting

Presentation of Gifts

Acknowledgments

Announcement of Winner

Murphy was front and center and as Murphy's Law worked, whatever could go wrong did go wrong.

It was important that the presentations go well and we reviewed those several times to work through the glitches.

It was the black tie affair of the year, even more illustrious than the Christmas ball, which I heard was the shindig not to miss.

I stretched my arms and got dressed as quickly as I could. I didn't plan to be in the office, but would spend my day covering last-minute confirmations with the entertainment, catering and my team to make sure we were all on the same page.

I met Rej at the conference entrance carrying a large package.

"What's that?" I asked.

"The big check," he smiled. "It finally arrived."

We had ordered the check way in advance but the first was damaged and the second somehow got lost in the mail. We were sure it wouldn't make it on time.

Everything seemed to be coming together. Nancy was already onsite putting together the remaining gift bags for the voter participants.

We would have a total of 55 pre-selected consumer voters, along with the original selection committee participating in the final vote. The system was set up where the selection committee's vote would have a heavier weight since it was only five of them.

After another long day of hard work, it was nearing time for us all to leave to go home to get dressed and the entertainment was still missing in action.

It was the current thorn in our sides.

"All we can do is pray they make it on time," I said. "I'll ask the event director if we can have sound and lighting support and you see if we can find a last minute DJ."

"Got it," Rej said.

I sat in one of the seats at the voting table and popped open my laptop. I connected to the conference hall's Wi-Fi and connected to Game Over's VPN.

I downloaded the latest version of my project schedule to make sure I wasn't forgetting anything important. I stared at the figure 95% complete, amazed at how far we had come.

I did a final review of the execution plan I had printed for my team members and we all left in our separate vehicles, wishing everyone well until a few hours when we would see each other again.

***

Returning to the conference hall in a tight-fitting black number my sister talked me into, I felt over-dressed for a night that would be filled with work.

Everyone looked amazing, and Rej's wife was more beautiful than her pictures. She thanked me in advance for approving Rej's time off after the project was officially closed out.

We completed our formal greetings and everyone took their seats as Blake was introduced to the crowd. Blake spoke as if he was giving his inaugural speech. He was certainly a natural on the stage and looked very comfortable introducing the candidates.

Each candidate was responsible for creating a presentation with highlights of their game demonstration. The candidates had done a good job of using their presentations as a buffer to showcase features they were unable to create in the demonstration.

The presentations were all very professional. I was heavily impressed with how Max and Rej came together to create sound and lighting effects that complemented each of the presentations.

The dancing lights and loud music had the crowd completely engaged and the convention center staff even stopped by to steal a look at the large screens.

Watching some of the presentations was similar to watching a trailer for a movie. It created a heightened anticipation for the possible release of the games.

The candidates, seated among family and friends, were all smiles and full of pride while witnessing their hard work.

I thought the selection committee did an excellent job at voting because from what I was witnessing, the consumer voters were going to have a hard time at the end of the night.

Two of the games were made to support Game Over's new 360 virtual goggles, while the others were renditions of sports and fighting games that I had never seen before.

"I need to speak with you," Matt whispered to me while I was smiling and talking with Charles who was my guest for the night.

"Noooo," I said, pleading with Matt that there wasn't an issue on our special night.

"Yeeess," Matt said, giving me a serious look. "The voting system has a glitch."

"Can I help?" Charles asked.

"Looks like it's time for voting and the system isn't working," I said, rising from my seat.

"Get your contact on the phone. Remember the on-call service I told you to reserve," Charles reminded me.

I pulled my work cell out of my clutch bag and I dialed the number that was listed on my execution plan under contacts.

I watched as the consumer group started to gather and I quickly handed Matt the phone to run through some troubleshooting before anyone noticed.

My eyes darted around the room, looking for Blake. It was important he remain in the world where everything was going perfectly.

He was back on stage, asking the entertainment for an encore.

"Uh huh, ok, got it." I could hear Matt taking orders from the voice on the other end of the phone.

I think Charles could see the nervousness in my demeanor and he placed a hand on my back and gave me a smile.

"Got it!" Matt jumped up and instructed the hired helpers on the necessary changes.

The voting was ready and the process went a lot faster than what we projected.

Nancy pitched in to help organize the voters and keep them occupied while they waited for an available voting unit.

One game in particular was standing out among the voters. It was evident right away as voters whispered their feedback into the crowd.

When the voting was complete, Blake took the stage once more and everyone took their seats for the last time.

Blake started his closing speech with thanks to the selection committee, offering them the gifts that Nancy and I had researched to no end to make him happy.

Blake even surprised me with a gift. It was a Game Over kudos pendant that was only distributed a couple of times a year by the CEO himself.

After Blake thanked our consumer voters, it was time for the announcement of the winning candidate.

Matt handed Blake an envelope with the computer-generated information that noted the winner within the confinements of the folded white paper.

Blake was very successful in taking a suspenseful long pause to open the envelope.

"And the winner is..." Blake smiled as everyone hung on each of his lingering words.

"Virtual Universe!" Blake screamed into the microphone beginning to clap immediately while inviting the winning team to the stage.

The entire team sprinted to the stage with excitement only seen in children on Christmas day. Each member of the team said words of thanks and the winning candidate was welcomed as a new member of the Game Over family.

The announcement ended the program and as the crowd began to disperse, I allowed myself a moment to take it all in and relax a little.

"You're still here?" I saw Charles walking up to me as I rubbed my aching feet.

"I had to congratulate you again," Charles said, shaking my hand.

"Well, trust me, you played a huge role in this success. I truly appreciate all that you have done to help me. You are truly the best mentor I have ever had," I said clambering to my feet.

"It was my pleasure," Charles smiled.

I gave Charles a big hug before we said our goodbyes.

I gazed at the room, proud of what I had accomplished and even more excited for what was to come.

15 THE CELEBRATION

"Tell us you have good news," Nancy said, smiling.

"This is the lessons learned meeting, not the good news session," I said, teasing.

"C'mon. You know you want to tell us," Rej said, poking me with his elbow.

Matt pretended to be interested as he looked up from his phone that resembled a mini tablet.

I sat silent for a little while longer, knowing they were anticipating my response.

"I passed!" I said, smiling as Nancy jumped from the floor. My announcement did not seem as unforgettable as Jessica's, but I was excited all the same.

"Way to go!" Matt said, almost sounding excited.

I believed Matt was truly happy for me; he was just not much for showing emotions.

"Sorry I had to postpone our Lessons Learned meeting for a couple of weeks, but I wanted to squeeze in my PMP exam before things got crazy with this kiosk project," I added.

"Trust me, we're good," Rej said, supporting my decision to take a break.

"So, let's talk about what went well," I said, getting the meeting started.

My agenda covered the highs, lows and opportunities for improvements. We also covered feedback from the programmers, candidates and the senior director of business development who were asked to complete an online survey.

Tracy interrupted our meeting briefly to congratulate us all on a job well done.

When the meeting ended, I thanked my team and asked if they were all ready to go.

"Ready to go?" Rej voiced everyone's confusion.

"Follow me," I said, leading them to one of the lounges where I had planned a small surprise luncheon for them and the programmers to celebrate and say thanks for all of their hard work.

Maggie and Ashli helped set up the decorations and even Jessica stopped by to lend a hand. Everything had turned out great and there was enough money left in the budget to provide gift cards for my team and the programmers.

"This is great," Bruce said, putting his hand on my shoulder.

I think he was more excited that his work was positively recognized for a change. Either way, it made for a much more comfortable working environment.

We talked and laughed and congratulated the candidate James, who was now an official Game Over member.

"You're one of us now," Bruce said, handing James a Game Over hat.

I mingled for a while before sneaking out of the

celebration to finish up last minute invoicing for the project. I was very close to completing the project closeout checklist and I was eager to finalize my work.

I smiled as I posted my final status report for the project. I was a smidge over my projected budget, bringing my total spending to $277,350.

I felt pretty good not going over my contingency spending and I hoped Blake would notice my good efforts.

I was ready to allocate more time to the kiosk project and whatever else Tracy would throw my way.

**

I closed my laptop and placed my framed PMP certificate on the hook on the wall.

It made me smile just to think of the accomplishment. Many hours of studying, long nights with coffee breaks and texts to Charles and a lot of sacrifices of *me* time.

I was headed out for my one-week vacation and it

was my intent to leave it all behind. Just as I thought of being completely free of Game Over, I dug in my handbag and pulled out my work phone. I placed it on top of my laptop, pulled my office door shut and locked the door.

There was one more thing I needed to do before I could fully enjoy my vacation, and that was hang out with my team.

We were meeting for tapas and drinks, at what had become our spot. We decided we needed our own celebration, together, after concluding what was our first official project.

As I entered the Happy Hour establishment I was greeted by the team.

"Hey, Joyce!" Nancy welcomed me with a smile.

Matt brought over a bottle of wine and we filled our glasses and lifted them high.

"What should we toast to?" I asked.

"Projects ending," Matt said.

"Vacation time," Rej added.

"New beginnings," Nancy smiled.

"I read something somewhere recently that I think is appropriate," I interrupted. "'May the work that you have be the play that you love.' You are the best group of people I have ever worked with and I enjoy sharing what I *love* to do with all of you. Thanks for a great project!"

"Not the mushy stuff," Matt said, smiling and taking a drink from his glass. He started to dance in his chair and we all joined in, exhibiting the excitement only a closed project could bring.

As I looked around the table at my team, I thought back to the first day and how it all began. We each had grown in our own way and closer together as a team.

My first project had been a success and while something told me they wouldn't all be that way, I marveled in the moment I shared with my team.

I had gone from a bored, unchallenged assistant to

a certified project manager at one of the top gaming firms in the country. *Not bad*, I thought. Not bad at all.

ABOUT THE AUTHOR

Dr. Arrington is an active PMI member, and serves as a project management and PMO implementation consultant, specializing in process improvement and change management. She also has a passion for teaching, and dedicates time instructing project management and marketing courses. She has an affinity for writing, and traveling with her two boys.